For Vicki —

Keep Strong!

Keith

Praise for Between the Notes

"Kevin is an immensely kind and wise person. That kind of wisdom only comes through lived life experience. He is sharing that life experience in this book. It contains universal and, at the same time, very personal principles. It is practical advice for managing this thing that we call life and steering your lifeboat in the direction of creativity, peace, and fulfillment. Bravo!"

—Stephanie Taylor MD, PhD

"Every person has a story inside them that must be told. For Kevin Roth, he had the courage to be transparent and share his life-changing journey in print. This inspiring book will help you discover hope and find sources of resilience to overcome the challenges you face in life. If you read it with an open heart and mind, it just might change your life."

—Rev. Dr. Brian Bohlman, Dulcimer Artist

"Love it! Best most concise rendering of hopeful I've read in a long time!"

—Noel Paul Stookey (Peter, Paul & Mary)

*"Kevin has a strong message to share with the world.
His story and life lessons are extremely powerful,
everyone should be able to hear them.
I am grateful he shared them with my audience."*

—Secrets of Designing Tomorrow Podcast Diana Popa

*"Kevin's insights are profound. There are
many great coaches out there, but rarely
amazing teachers. Kevin is both."*

—Steve Garjohn, Coaching Client

BETWEEN THE NOTES

Practical Ways to Find Your **INNER GROOVE** and **DANCE** to a Beat That Makes Your **HEART SING**

KEVIN ROTH

Disclaimer

The author is providing this book and its contents on an "as is" basis and makes no representations or warranties of any kind with respect to this book or its contents. The author disclaims all such representations and warranties, including but not limited to warranties of healthcare for a particular purpose. In addition, the author assumes no responsibility for errors, inaccuracies, omissions, or any other inconsistencies herein. The purpose of this book is to educate. It is not a replacement for medical advice.

BETWEEN THE NOTES

Practical Ways to Find Your Inner Groove and Dance to a Beat That Makes Your Heart Sing

Kevin Roth

GLOBAL WELLNESS MEDIA
STRATEGIC EDGE INNOVATIONS PUBLISHING
LOS ANGELES, TORONTO, MONTREAL

First Edition. Published by:
Global Wellness Media
Strategic Edge Innovations Publishing
340 S Lemon Ave #2027
Walnut, California 91789-2706
(866) 467-9090
StrategicEdgeInnovations.com

Publisher's Note: The views expressed in this work are solely those of the authors and do not necessarily reflect the views of the publisher, and the publisher hereby disclaims any responsibilities for them.

Editors: Sarah Aschenbach, Shannon O'Keeffe
Book Design: Global Wellness Media

Between the Notes / Kevin Roth. -- 1st ed.
ISBN: 978-1-957343-08-2 (Paperback)
ISBN: 978-1-957343-09-9 (ePub)

Table of Content

Section 1

THE JOURNEY

Section 2

EPIPHANIES AND AHA! MOMENTS

Section 3

PRACTICAL WAYS TO LIVE IN THE GROOVE

Dedication

This book is dedicated to those who are weary, lost, and stuck, those who feel there is no way out of their abyss. Trust me, the saying that it is often darkest before the dawn is true. I assure you, there is a way out of the darkness and into the light.

In memory of my friend and teacher,
Robert Wolfe.

Acknowledgments

Thank you to Rosalie, Missy, Sharon, Bob, Jyll, Beth, Noel, Ron, Anne, James, Jerry, Mitchell, Roy, and Stephanie for your insights.

Thanks to all my students and clients who have given me the privilege and opportunity of working with you to discover a happier life. You've brought joy into mine.

Many thanks to Shannon O'Keeffe of Manifestability.com for helping to develop the content and to Sarah Aschenbach of Inspired Solutions, whose line editing brought it all home.

Thanks A Latte

He pours a heart in my coffee
The liquid artist knows my brew
I'm sitting on the couch in the coffee shop
Just being, thinking of you
I was hiking in the mountains
And listening to my heart
I know what we had is gone,
so with love I'm moving on
It's time for a brand-new start

Every day's a new day, you get another chance
To get it right, and find your inner groove
And like nobody's watching—DANCE

Folks on laptops, headphones,
scrolling on their cellphones
Texting their life away
Everybody's searching for love
and sweet connections
At the end of the day
I may be alone but I'm rarely lonely
I guess I've come to realize
I'm good sitting with my Doxie at Thanks A Latte

Just watching the world go by

I've got a romantic date with Moi tonight
I like hanging with myself sometimes
Tonight, its coq au vin *with lights dimmed low*
And a smoky bottle of wine
I'll spin Nina Simone (moan, moan, moan)
With a goblet of cabernet
I hope that the muse shows up a little later
And comes on out to play

Words and music by Kevin Roth.

Introduction

One New Year's Eve back in my mid-twenties I was in Portland, Maine, on a concert tour, depressed as hell. I had just performed a concert where everyone was celebrating. I, on the other hand, was alone, in a city where I knew no one, and it was New Year's Eve. Maine was nearly seven below zero, which gave the expression "when hell freezes over" a new meaning. I went to a diner; as I sat by myself, a hefty waitress poured me a cup of coffee, and we began to talk. It was a moment of talking to a stranger I would never see again about anything at all. I poured my heart out. She followed with her own tales to a stranger. Then, the diner was closing, and she asked me to go dancing at an all-night dance club. "I can't dance," I told her when we arrived, and she said, "C'mon, nobody knows you here." Under flashing strobe lights, we had some drinks. She literally bounced me off her huge hips on purpose as we danced and laughed our asses off to Gloria Gaynor's "I Will Survive." For the first time in my life, I danced like nobody was watching. I didn't know the waitress's name, and it didn't matter. We were strangers in love with being strangers, confessing stories of ordinary madness, and for a few hours, we lived out loud.

I remembered that story nearly thirty-five years later when I received the frightening news that I had stage-three melanoma and a 70 percent chance of dying within two years. Since that evening of dancing in Maine, all the years in between were spent building a half-hearted career, being a slave to my stock portfolio, and searching in all the wrong places for deeper meaning in life. Remembering the waitress and Gloria Gaynor singing "I Will Survive," I decided it was time to put on my dancing shoes and live out loud again. It was time to survive.

In 2015, after my doctor told me that I had stage-three melanoma, I hung up the phone and sat on my couch, stunned, and trembling with fear. I felt a total lack of control over what was going on in my own body. It felt like a personal invasion on every level I could imagine. The only way I could regain any sense of control was to begin to explore three major questions:

- What really matters to me?

- Why does it matter to me?

- What the hell am I going to do about it?

The answers I found, and which I share in this book, led to the biggest epiphanies of my life. You learn a lot about yourself when you hit bottom. Through dealing with cancer, I discovered that I'm a brave son of a bitch. I can take a hit. I didn't know I had it in me until I looked back at my life while writing this book. I guess that's how I made it in the music business and life. Guts and glory.

In Charles Bukowski's poem, "The Laughing Heart," he writes, "You can't beat death, but you can beat death in life sometimes. And the more often you learn to do it, the more light there will be."

Well, I ended up beating cancer and depression and winning the subtle war of searching for happiness that had frustrated me for most of my life. I finally learned how to surrender to an innovative, fun, and creative life in California, and I love it. Every day, I create my own story in life, and like Sinatra, I do it my way. Every morning I sit with a cup of fresh-ground coffee, playing my dulcimer, a beautiful American folk stringed instrument, and think about what matters to me and why it matters. I intentionally create the kind of day I want to experience. I call this *Kevin's Creative Life Design.* Everything I do throughout the day supports my life choices, my health, and my happiness. Having created my story, I walk into it like an actor playing a part in a movie. I choose to stay as far away from stress, drama, and negativity as possible and I rely on mindful awareness as I navigate my way through life's ups and downs.

Before cancer, whenever I heard someone say that the lessons cancer taught them were gifts, I did not believe them; probably because I hadn't had that experience. Now, I can honestly tell you this: as horrible an experience as cancer is, it completely changed my life for the better, and the lessons I learned are the ones I now share with people around the world.

This book is about discovering hope and navigating life's choices. I'll share with you what worked for me during my own "awakening" process and what I now teach others: you, too, can create your own story in which you are living the authentic, happy, and complete life you've longed for.

Although my story is unique to me, it may resonate with you. I've always agreed with the saying that we are spiritual beings having a human experience. How we choose to live this experience is mostly up to us. In my own way, I've learned how to be "in this world but not of it."

I invite you to create a life you love from what I've learned and from others whose wisdom I share. It continues to change my life, to bring me success and joy, and to inspire me to dance like nobody's watching.

Section 1

THE JOURNEY

Chapter 1

There's Nothing Like a Death Sentence to Wake You Up

"The good thing about bad situations is that they allow you to see how good you are at overcoming them."
—Unknown

There comes a time for most people when they experience a difficult and painful period in life that in some traditions is known as the dark night of the soul. It's when you hit bottom and think you may never see your way out of the abyss. Mine came while I was living in Florida in 2014. During that year, my father—who was my best friend—passed away, my small retail store nearly bankrupted me, and my nine-year relationship ended. I had been living in the Fort Lauderdale area for fifteen years by then, and, based on a precognitive experience I had one evening, I decided to move to Kansas to hang out with my sister until I figured out my future.

Two months after arriving in Kansas, during a routine dermatology appointment, the doctor pointed out a small dark freckle on my nose. He took a scraping, and the following week, he sent me to a plastic surgeon for a biopsy. The result came back as *in situ*, which means that it was not quite cancer. It was determined that I needed to have Mohs surgery performed so that nothing further would develop. As I looked into the mirror after the surgery and saw a black eye and bandages across my nose, I thought, "Well, at least it isn't cancer."

The pathology report was wrong. Three months later, while shaving, I found a lump under my chin. My instinct told me I was in trouble. I was sent to an ENT doctor for a needle biopsy, followed shortly afterward by a surgery to remove a lymph node. I waited nearly two long weeks for the results. In my apartment, staring at a photo of my father on a Sunday evening, as if he were in the room, I heard him say, "Kev, you're going to hear tomorrow, and it's going to be bad news. You'll be okay, but it's going to be very rough." The next morning at nine o'clock, the doctor called. As my father had warned me, the doctor told me I needed to see an oncologist immediately.

I had stage 3 melanoma. I walked through my apartment in a daze and said aloud, "Don't worry, buddy, we'll get through this." At first, I didn't know who I was talking to. Suddenly, there were two of me. That's when I realized that this was the first time in my life that I had seen myself as my own best friend. For most of my life, I had been focused on the next business deal and hadn't taken much time to enjoy my accomplishments. Now, my entire focus was on staying alive.

That year, while living in Kansas with this sudden new prognosis, turned into something out of a sci-fi horror movie. I became part of the "C" world. Cancer was something that I thought happened to other people, certainly not me. I had worked out, eaten mostly healthy foods, I didn't smoke, and now—out of the blue—I had to find an oncologist. The search for an oncologist I trusted was arduous. I met several, but my gut said, *"Run!"* I finally found one doctor, Dr. G, whom my instincts told me was the guy to go to, but when I called his office, I was told he was not accepting any new patients. Because I needed further testing to see if the melanoma had spread anywhere else, I ended up with a doctor I did not like, but she was able to schedule the MRI and CAT scans I needed.

The morning I went to her office to get the test results, I was petrified. She sat emotionless while reading me the results from her computer screen. The cancer had not spread, she informed me, but I needed a lymphadenectomy. I was shocked. Why? I asked her, if there was no sign of cancer in my body, why should I have my lymph nodes removed? She told me it was "protocol."

"My name is not protocol!" I left her office angry, but then I noticed a card on the receptionist's desk with Dr. G's name on it, the doctor I had originally wanted to see. I asked the receptionist if Dr. G worked there. She said yes, but he was not taking any new patients. I insisted on seeing him and got an appointment for the following morning.

Dr. G was *the only* oncologist out of all the ones I had seen that agreed with me that I should not do anything.

9

"There is no cure," he told me. There was also a 70 percent chance the melanoma would return within a year. If that happened, he said, I'd probably be dead within two or three years.

That year was a horrible waiting game, full of fear and deep reflection. It was really a spiritual kick in my ass. I'm here to tell you, there's nothing like a death sentence to wake you up.

***

Many songs I've written throughout my music career reflect my search for love and deeper meaning in life. During the writing of this book, certain songs came back to me as a reflective retrospection and reminder of my journey. *Rain Walker* reflects the loneliness of going through hard times while knowing there's always a shoulder to lean on.

Rain Walker

Come in, come in, come in out of the rain
You don't need to explain where you've been
I can see by the look in your eyes,
you've been running wild
You're at the end of your line

And you know I won't ask anything of you
Take all the time you need to pull yourself through

THERE'S NOTHING LIKE A DEATH SENTENCE...

You can cry—go and cry if you need to
You can laugh if you feel you
need to balance your soul
There's a fire in the stove and tea on the table
I know a prayer that will stabilize
any storm that grows cold

There's a room in the morning that brings in the sun
I go there sometimes to start the day
There are books on the shelves filled
with wisdom and laughter
For the mornings after I lose my way

I'll be here if you need someone to talk to
Or someone to hold you and play you a song
I've been there where you are a thousand times over
A Rain Walker, a rover, wondering where I belong

Words and music by Kevin Roth.

Chapter 2
Realization

*"When the student is ready
the teacher appears."*
—Tao Te Ching

Wheard the news of my potential early
demise, I thought about my life and what I
would have done differently if only I had known
it would be cut short. I had done enough research to know
that stress and inflammation were two of the leading causes
of cancer, and I understood how both had played a huge
part in my illness. As I prepared myself for surgery, I
considered the changes I needed to make.

Stress

I had lived with stress for most of my life as I dealt with the
fallout of being raised in a dysfunctional family where
personal boundaries and unconditional love were hard to
come by. Fortunately, I'd had the wisdom to put myself
through psychotherapy in my early twenties, where I was
able to resolve many of those feelings. It was one of the
greatest gifts I ever gave myself. Even so, I had
experienced ongoing stress for most of my life, chasing

happiness as I tried to make it in the music business and pay the bills. I could see that stress had played a big part in my life. I saw that it was part of the recipe that had allowed melanoma to emerge. Since I couldn't go back in time and change these things, I knew I had to make shifts in my life as I moved forward.

Inflammation

Unfortunately, my mother was an emotional eater, and she passed her coping mechanism to me. Like her, I used food to numb the pain in life. Although I was never obese, I had struggled with weight for most of my life. Remarkably, I never got into alcohol or drugs, which many musicians used as their means of coping. I realize my emotional eating of unhealthy foods, especially sugars and refined carbohydrates, had created inflammation in my body.

Constant Pursuit of Happiness

I could see that my constant pursuit of happiness was making me miserable. I had come to understand that everything I thought would make me happy—money, being famous, and "stuff"—was as fleeting as fame itself. It was a cause of stress in my life, and not worth the price I was now paying.

Revelations

Teachers come in many forms and show up when we are ready for true change. I had three major revelations that fundamentally changed my life.

14

Self-realization is crucial to a happy life.

As if finding Dr. G hadn't been incredible enough, one day shortly after my Mohs surgery, I saw a documentary on Netflix called *Awake*. It was about Yogananda, an Indian guru who taught self-realization. I wasn't particularly interested in him, but my gut told me to watch the film. I did, and afterward, I had a strong impulse to google and see where one of his fellowships was located. I was sure I would never find one in Kansas, but I knew there were one or two in California. I was astonished to find that there was a fellowship just a quarter mile away from my apartment. I couldn't believe it. I went to a Saturday morning service, and although I didn't understand what all the chanting was about, I felt a huge feeling of relief, as if all my burdens had been lifted off my shoulders. I began to read his books and found great peace, but I never felt that Yogananda was my spiritual teacher; however, I did gain an understanding of what self-realization was about. According to Yogananda, self-realization is "The knowing—in body, mind, and soul—that we are one with the omnipresence of God."

Through my curiosity to delve deeper into self-realization, I came across an author by the name of Robert Wolfe, who had written a book about a sage from India, Ramana Maharshi. As soon as I began to read Ramana's teachings, I knew I had found what I had been looking for. His teachings were clear and simple, and he gave instructions on how to go about understanding who I truly was. Like when I discovered the dulcimer, a musical

15

instrument that became my career path, it was a huge Aha! moment.

I needed to find a survivor of melanoma.

While I was devouring Ramana's work, I also was searching for someone who had lived through melanoma without major drugs or surgery and had been cured. I found Prudence Sinclair. Prudence was diagnosed with stage 4 melanoma and had been told she would be dead within six months. She had proven the doctors wrong. She cured herself with meditation, healthy food, and an amazingly determined and positive attitude.

Prudence has been cancer-free for over twenty years. She helped me understand epigenetics and was a guide for me through a most difficult time. I knew others had tried traditional treatments, coffee enemas, and treatment centers in Mexico to help them, but my gut told me to stay with the guidance of Prudence and Dr. G.

I needed to drop negativity.

The third revelation was the need to rid my environment of negativity immediately. I had to drop stress, and that included avoiding negative people and ridding myself of stinkin' thinkin.' Dropping negativity sounds relatively simple, but first, I realized that I needed to know what deeply matters to me on a soul level, why it matters, and what I was going to do about it.

What Mattered and What to Do About It

What mattered to me? My music, art, spirituality, and my dog, Bosco. It was not money or fame, and yet I had poured my heart and energy into seeking them for most of my life. Why did music, art, spirituality, and Bosco matter to me? Because at heart I am a musician and an artist, I am spiritual, and my dog Bosco is my soul fur-mate.

Once I knew what mattered most to me, what was I going to do about it? Well, first, I needed to drop the victim story I had created for myself over the years and then write a new story. I was determined that I was going to beat cancer, leave Kansas and move to sunny California, and create a fun, creative, successful, and amazing life I loved. No more stress, feeling stuck, and living in fear.

By becoming crystal-clear on what truly mattered and going for it, I was able to create a life design that felt authentic, practical, freeing, and fun. It remains the cornerstone of my life to this day. Along with mindful awareness, healthy eating, exercise, and maintaining a hopeful and positive outlook, it has helped to strengthen my immunity and fight off illnesses.

The guidance I received from Dr. G and Prudence Sinclair, along with my spiritual reading, gradually reshaped my thinking. My soul wanted to be a bohemian musician and artist. The role I had been playing was that of a half-hearted musician and business guy. The two no longer matched. I had to find a way to blend my role with my soul, and that involved having a little chat with myself. It was a very brief conversation that went like this: "Kevin, from now on, you're going to live authentically, do what you love, love what you do, and have faith that it's all going to work out." I was beginning to completely trust my inner-guidance system.

The new story I created was that of a lean, mean, creative machine. I was replacing fear with faith and "going for it." I felt excited about my life again. I sensed that a new me was about to emerge. I saw myself writing songs, painting, and creating a life I loved. My gut told me that if I were true to myself, the money would flow, happiness would grow, and my role and my soul would become "One."

Finding the Right Environment

Living in Kansas was not ideal for me, so towards the end of the first year after my diagnosis, I decided to move back to San Diego. When I discussed my move to California with Dr. G, he suggested I have a CT scan before I leave.

"Why?" I asked.

"To see if there are any new signs of cancer so you can plan your life."

"What life? This past year was hardly what I'd call a life, at least not one I am willing to experience again. I'm going to move to California, and if I end up getting sick, so be it. At least in California, there is an end-of-life option. They don't have that in Kansas. Since there are no cures, and I am feeling healthy, I'm going to head west without any more scans."

He smiled. He advised me to get plenty of rest, to see a dermatologist, and if I felt sick or showed any concerning signs in the future, he would recommend a doctor in San Diego.

I contacted my friend Steve, a realtor who lived in San Diego, and asked if he could help me find a one-bedroom apartment for a thousand dollars a month. He laughed and told me I couldn't even find a studio for that price.

I wasn't going to let that stop me. No. I envisioned myself:

- Cancer-free

- Living in a one-bedroom apartment

- Living near the ocean

- Paying a thousand dollars a month, parking and laundry included

This was nearly impossible to come by in San Diego. I called around for two weeks and finally found an apartment for exactly one thousand dollars that was being redone and would be ready at the beginning of May, just three months away! My vision had become a reality. The process of making my new life happen was similar to the way I had created my music career:

I saw it, felt it, and walked into it!

On May 3, 2016, I packed my jeep with dulcimers, a few original paintings, and clothes. With Bosco in his bed on the passenger seat, I drove for three days in what seemed like a daze into my new life. It was a new beginning. Best of all, I've remained cancer-free.

Two quotes became my mantras. The first expresses how I felt while going through my existential crisis. In the movie, *The Shawshank Redemption*, Andy, played by Tim Robbins, says to his friend, Red, played by Morgan Freeman: "I guess it comes down to a simple choice, really. Get busy living or get busy dying." I chose the former.

The second mantra is from Emile Zola: "If you ask me what I came into this life to do, I will tell you: I came to live out loud."

I had been through a type of metamorphous during my year in Kansas. Now, I was ready to emerge like a butterfly and soar through the sunny skies of San Diego.

***

The Butterfly Boy

*He was in his cocoon, wrapped up and
immune to living the dream in the sky
You could see in his eyes, the look of surprise
when he suddenly learned he could fly
Discovering himself, he became something else,
his enigma he never had known
Feeling vibrations in each situation,
he discovered a world of his own*

With his butterfly wings
and the song the wind sings,
he was musical art flying high
Landing on flowers for hours and hours
lived the butterfly boy in the sky

The look on his face showed surrender
and grace as the epiphany came to eyes
Once his body was spreading,
now it was shedding,
like watercolor rain from the sky
Oh, everything changes, life rearranges,
nothing is quite what it seems
On his last day, in a colorful blaze,
he flew right into his next dream.

He was a pallet of colors from one wing
to the other like Monet taking flight
He painted each scene
as he flew through his dream,
going gently into the night.

Words and music by Kevin Roth.

Chapter 3
Rags to Riches Doesn't Equal Happiness

"Having money doesn't make you happy, it just makes being miserable more comfortable."
—Johnny Carson

A h, the American dream! I thought if only I became rich and famous, my life would be set. I'd have everything I needed and be happy as a clam.

From as far back as I can remember, I wanted a major record deal, a hit, a book deal, a TV show—I'd be able to take my musical whims on the road and there'd be performances in beautiful concert halls that culminated in standing ovations. Isn't that every musician's dream? It took time, but it all happened for me, and just like other dreamers who want to become doctors, successful investors, entrepreneurs, or even the toast of high society, I can tell you these things take time, have a high cost, and never end up being what you thought they'd be. Many of my friends who became doctors have questioned in hindsight whether they made the right choice, citing medical bureaucracy, pharma propaganda problems, and, of course, stress, to name a few downsides. Very few musicians stay at the top, and most have lost their fortunes on the way back down. I never even made it to the top, yet I became well enough known in folk music and family entertainment circles to open doors, make deals, and grow my career.

The truth is, when I was a child, the only validation and praise I received was for my musical abilities. I had problems in school because I was dyslexic, and my home life was beyond dysfunctional, so it was only natural to gravitate towards what I was good at and what felt nurturing to me and those who heard my music. I was extremely fortunate to discover the dulcimer at the age of thirteen, and then at sixteen to sign my first record deal with Folkways Records in 1974. I created a dozen albums over a decade that are now part of The Smithsonian Folkways Records label. The bottom line is: music saved me.

I became known in folk music as an innovative dulcimer player and singer. I never could find a decent agent or manager, so I ended up being my own booking agent, a job I hated. I booked folk festivals, clubs, and a few decent-size venues, but there wasn't much of a living to be made in folk music unless you were Peter, Paul & Mary, Judy Collins, or Joan Baez and had millions of fans and hit records.

On a whim, I heard that children's music was becoming popular so, in 1984, I made my first recording for children, and it became the flagship for my own record label. It was called *Lullabies for Little Dreamers*. It sold very well and launched a career for me in kids' music that I never saw coming. I had caught the wave of the dulcimer's popularity in the 1970s, and now I had caught the wave of children's and family music.

I always loved writing and recording children's music, but I didn't like performing for kids because the littlest children like to sing nursery rhymes and songs they know. They have little patience for unfamiliar material with adult, soul-searching themes, which is what I wanted to write and sing. I rectified this early in my children's songwriting career by writing about love, hope, and adult feelings using the subject matter of bears, trains, and other whimsical characters, often with humor and a twist. Although to some degree this worked beautifully, I still felt musically demoted.

From time to time, though, amazing things happened that reminded me that my music and life path were not all about my ego and my career choices.

Marti's Song

One day, something happened that affected me so deeply that I never forgot it. A woman came backstage five minutes before I was about to walk on stage to give a children's concert. She handed me a folded flyer. "I hope you don't mind, Mr. Roth, but my daughter Marti loved your music and went to bed each night with your song, "Lullaby Bears," from your Unbearable Bears album, so I printed the lyrics to that song inside her funeral program. We played your recording during her service. I just wanted to thank you and let you know how much your music meant to her."

I had never gotten choked up before a concert, and honestly, I was amazed that I could even go on. That experience alone made me realize how much music can affect people's lives, especially the lives of young children. Every song I wrote for children always included a subtle message of love in one form or another. When I reprinted that album, I changed the title of the song to *Marti's Song/Lullaby Bears* in her honor.

What Kids Taught Me

This time in my life was also the beginning of questioning myself: Why was I often annoyed by singing for children? (Other than because I wasn't crazy about the type of music.)

Children are very needy by nature. I was needy, too, but because my needs were never met in a healthy way when I was a child, when I saw children acting crazy and needy at my shows, it pushed a button in me. When kids didn't always pay attention to me on stage or acted up during a concert just like I did as a child, I felt dismissed. Years later, after I had worked through those feelings, I found children very entertaining.

Children also occasionally gave me reality checks. A kid once came up to me after a show and asked me if I was famous. "Well, have you ever heard of me?" I asked him.

"No."

"I guess not then," I replied.

26

My favorite reality check came when I quickly scribbled my autograph on an album because I was in a hurry to leave. When I gave it back to the kid, he said, "Look, Mom, Kevin's learning to write, too." But by far the biggest reality check came years after I had stopped recording children's music: I discovered how moved I am when someone tells me they grew up listening to my music. Am I really that old? Ha!

I continued writing children's albums. I gave as many concerts as I could to pay the bills. I was glad I was able to make a comfortable living, something I was not able to do as a folk singer. Looking back now, I can see I was lucky to have had a good and successful run, despite my wanting to be Mr. Joni Mitchell.

The Big Break

In 1988, I received a phone call from Rick Siggelkow, who was producing a show for PBS called *Shining Time Station*, based on *Thomas the Tank Engine*. The big star of the show was Ringo, from The Beatles, who played the conductor.

Rick had been putting his daughter to bed with my lullaby album each night, and he thought I'd be perfect to sing the theme song. *Shining Time Station* became an instant television hit, and suddenly my voice was heard by millions around the country. As if overnight, I became well known. I could now call any major concert hall and book myself as a children's performer based on the show's popularity. Suddenly, I was making big bucks for just one hour of singing instead of a few hundred for an entire evening at some folk club.

Because I owned my own records, publishing company, and rights, I was in the position to negotiate licensing deals with major companies, such as Sony Music, Random House, Book of The Month Club, and many others who were eager to have me as part of their catalog. My children's music career was flying high. I was invited to perform at The White House twice for the Easter Egg Roll event, sharing the stage with Shari Lewis and Lambchop; Peter, Paul & Mary; and others. Many of my musical heroes now knew who I was. It was astonishing.

By the time I was thirty-five, due to smart investments, I became a millionaire. It was sweet while it lasted, but there was a big caveat: Although I had a lot of zeros in my checking account, I had one big fat zero in my soul because people wanted me to sing children's songs and I didn't want to. People were not taking me seriously as an adult singer-songwriter any longer. I felt like I had been cast as a children's singer, and that would remain my fate.

Riches to Rags

I was living in California in the late nineties, thinking I could just kick back and not sing for a while and life would be great. Then, the dot-com bubble burst and stocks took a dive. I lost a lot of money. Frightened, I sold my house and bought a villa in Florida. My father lived there, we were close, and it was much cheaper to live in Florida than in California.

I invested the money I had left in the real estate market and was doing very well until a few years later when it, too, crashed.

My Perfect Storm

One of my favorite books is *The Perfect Storm*, about a storm that hit North America in 1991. The men and their fishing boat, the Andrea Gail, were caught in one of the worst weather events in New England history. They were lost at sea during severe conditions while fishing 575 miles out to sea.

In 2014, my own perfect storm began to brew. My father passed away, my nine-year relationship ended, and a little artsy-looking store I had opened the previous year while taking a hiatus from the music business nearly put me into bankruptcy. I felt mentally and emotionally bankrupt, as well. Now, I had to return to making a living. What should I do?

Being in the music business was no longer making me happy. My music was being downloaded from the internet for practically nothing. Along with other artists, I experienced the fallout. My CD sales plummeted, and the small fees musicians were receiving for downloads didn't even amount to enough to cover bills. If you were a touring musician, you could sell merchandise at the concerts, but gigs were hard to get because of the economy of that time. Everything that had meant something special to me in the past seemed gone.

Burnt-out, I quit the music business and became an abstract painter. However, I kept my eye out for the next wave I could catch to take me back to my soul on shore.

In February of 2014, I walked into my apartment feeling very depressed. "What do I really want in my life?" The answer became crystal-clear. I wanted to be spiritually enlightened. Three months later, I left Florida and went to live with my sister in Kansas until I figured out my next step in life.

**

Marti's Song/Lullaby Bears

Little bears are dancing
round and round
When I sleep, they always come around
Fuzzy bears, cuddly bears,
jumping up and down
My lullaby, lullaby bears

Come lay your head down gently next to me
Let the world of dreaming set you free
Dancing round and round
Sleeping oh so soundly,
lullaby, lullaby bears.

Taffy dreams with wings up in the sky
Angels come and hold me as I lie

RAGS TO RICHES DOESN'T EQUAL HAPPINESS

Dream of peace my child,
let the Lord hold you
In lullaby, lullaby bears

Words and music by Kevin Roth.

Chapter 4
Precognition and Out-of-Body Experiences

"The most beautiful experience we can have is the mysterious."
—Albert Einstein

Being diagnosed with melanoma shouldn't have surprised me. In fact, it was foretold to me as a young boy how my life would unfold, and again as an adult in the form of precognition and out-of-body (OBE) experiences while I was living in Florida.

I was the type of child who wondered about the nature of the cosmos and tried to make sense of the universe. When I asked adults about such things, I was always led to science or God.

Science

Most adults and teachers pointed me in the direction of science for the answers I was seeking. I looked, and science didn't explain how the universe came to be; it was just how they *thought* the universe worked.

God

When science couldn't tell me what I wanted to know, I was pointed to God. I was told that God created the world in six days and took a breather on the seventh. Why would God need to rest? Did he/she get tired? That made no sense to me, either.

Psychics and Astrologers

As I got older, I discovered psychics and astrologers, and I thought they might have a clue about life's mysteries. Maybe they could explain what my experiences meant, and how to make sense of it all. Most weren't able to do that, but I met a few who gave me incredibly accurate readings about my life. How could another human being, someone I'd never met, know that I would end up singing for children and appear on TV? I had zero interest in any of that at the time.

My cousin, Sylvia Sherman, was a superb astrologer. When I was in my late twenties, she told me that when I was in my mid-fifties, I would have a great many health and emotional issues. I recalled that conversation a year or so after I got through my melanoma drama. Some might explain that these were simply ideas planted in my subconscious; I believed them and, in some way, I made them happen. My answer to them is to talk to me after you've had any of these experiences, yourself. Then you can look me in the face and tell me that I made them happen.

I'm the kind of person who must experience something firsthand before I believe it. I'm not easily swayed, but I can't deny many experiences that have occurred in my life. You can't *unknow* what you *know*. Having seen many of my precognitive experiences turn out to be accurate, I couldn't deny that something was going on that was far beyond what most consider "normal."

Spiritual Exploration

As I explored spirituality, I came to understand that who and what I am is not just this body, but something so immense that there are no words to describe it. It's like trying to explain where the mind is located. You can dissect a brain and never find something called a mind to hold in your hand, yet we all talk about the mind and assume that we have one, and that's just the way it is.

My father often asked me, "Why do you even think about these things?"

"Because life doesn't make sense or seem logical to me," I told him. "Why and how are we born? Where do we come from? And where do we go when we die?"

He'd make a face. "People have sex and then babies are born. You live and then you die. What difference does it make? Just live your life, work, be a good person, and enjoy yourself—I don't know why you're always searching for some explanation about life!"

We'd look at each other like we were both nuts.

The funny thing is, we were both artists, and we were especially close. Since he, too, was an artist, I believe he thought about such things but didn't dwell on them. Once when we were in synagogue, I asked him if he believed in God. He shrugged his shoulders as if to say, "Meh."

"If you're not sure, then why do you come here?"

"Just in case," he replied.

He kept life simple. In a sense, he lived his life as if he were a Buddhist without knowing it, a true "Jewbu." On the other hand, I felt I had no choice but to explore these questions and seek answers. Music and spirituality are the marrow of my being.

Precognitive and Out-of-Body Experiences

Precognitive experiences and OBEs are as natural to me as composing music, and I've had them all my life.

According to Wikipedia, precognition is the purported psychic phenomenon of seeing, or otherwise becoming directly aware of, events in the future. An OBE is an experience involving a feeling of separation from one's body and the ability to see oneself and others from an external perspective. Occasionally, I also have out-of-body experiences that also involve a precognitive experience.

Many doctors, clergy, nurses, scientists, and people from around the world have had precognitive, out-of-body, and near-death experiences, and these have been documented in numerous scientific papers and books.

Now, *precognitive*, *OBE*, and *NDE* (near-death experience) are just terms. Whether you see the experiences as energy, awareness, consciousness, God, or something else, there is no way to accurately describe what is happening or how it works. The experience doesn't make logical sense in the relative world.

Many people doubt that these experiences are real, and yet I believe we all have experiences that can't be logically explained, and yet we accept them as "normal" and "real." For instance, as a young boy, how was I able to hear music and then play it on the piano without knowing anything about reading music? How can an artist who has absolutely no training in portraiture be able to create one that looks lifelike? Savants are another great example of human experiences for which there is no logical explanation.

I was approximately seven years old when I had my first precognitive experience. It was like watching coming attractions in a movie, except that I was seeing my future. The experience felt very natural, just like my ability to play the piano by ear. During that childhood experience, I saw three phases of my life.

Precognitive Experience of My First Phase of Life
In the first phase, I saw myself going through childhood. I was having difficulty understanding what I was doing here on earth and getting along with other people. Looking back at that period, I remember I always felt like an old soul and was uncomfortable around kids my age. Later on, my sister reflected that I was always an overly perceptive kid. I always felt like I didn't belong here, as if I had been dropped off at a summer school I didn't want to attend. I was aware of a substratum, an all-embracing power that felt as close to me as my own self yet distant at the same time.

When I started to play the piano by ear at the age of four or five, I wondered where all the music came from.

Precognitive Experience of My Second Phase of Life

The second phase was my middle-age period. I saw that my life would be a struggle on emotional, mental, and spiritual levels, but I'd be successful in business. True enough, in that next phase, there was much turmoil. I was beginning to become more aware that life is an illusion. I felt disconnected from the relative world and more connected to the spiritual. It was like having one foot in each world. And I was quite successful in business.

Powerful precognitive experiences stay with you for a lifetime. That's why I always knew I was going to make it in the music business. My entire life was about my career. I felt like I had a destiny, and I was going to fulfill it one way or the other.

Precognitive Experience of the Final Phase of My Life

This is the most challenging phase to explain. I saw that this would be a time of spiritual longing in which I would come to understand what this life is about, and I would finally be happy. I saw, too, that I would have something to do with an eclectic form of higher learning and teaching.

The phases that were revealed to me have become a reality that continues to unfold.

The one unexpected thing I didn't visualize in the final phase of life, as shown in my OBE, was becoming a teacher of spirituality. Now, I understand how it has come to pass.

In my work as a teacher and personal life coach, I help people rewrite their life stories. I always teach about spirituality, because it goes hand-in-hand with how people find meaning in their lives. Sometimes things do come to pass in ways that are unexpected.

When I was fifty-seven and living in Florida, I had another precognitive experience. I saw myself moving to Kansas and living near my sister. I also saw that I'd survive a major illness and then move back to California, feeling free and happy.

I believe people are curious about precognitive, out-of-body, and near-death experiences. More people than you may imagine have had these experiences and talked about them. Earlier, people were afraid to talk about their experiences, fearing they would be judged, but now we know that millions of people around the world have similar experiences. The experiences are different, unique to each person, and now, finally, we are sharing them with others privately and in public. The word is out.

***

Come with Me

I'm caught between two worlds
in the matrix of my mind
I want to leave it all behind, come with me

39

You cannot comprehend when
the mind wants to pretend
There's no beginning or no end,
come with me

When you know too much
you can't go back there
When you feel the rush,
there's nothing to compare
So, you just let go and slowly
you become aware
That all you really care about is love

I closed my eyes and dreamed
of an astral plane it seems
Where everything was brighter than the sun
In joy I laughed and cried,
a part of me had died
And I saw love in everyone

I was lost between two worlds
in the matrix of my mind
I had to leave it all behind, come with me
And ever since that day
when I felt that brilliant blaze
I've been awakened and now I'm free

Words and music by Kevin Roth.

Chapter 5
Awakening, Coincidences, and Synchronicity

"Fix your course on a star and you'll
navigate any storm."
—Leonardo da Vinci

They say that timing is everything. When I look back at certain events in my life and their timing, I can see an almost mystical thread woven through them. There really are no coincidences in life. When I was first diagnosed with melanoma, I thought my world was coming to an end. I had no idea that my "year of fear" and everything I went through would be the catalyst for a new version—of not only my life but of my music career as well. I would help people navigate through their own difficulties and create a life they love.

A most amazing "coincidence" happened just two weeks after I left Florida to live in Kansas. I was told that Peter Yarrow and Noel Paul Stookey of Peter, Paul & Mary (PP&M) were performing at a local theater in a few days. I couldn't believe it. The timing was eerie. I had become close friends with PP&M, but I had not seen Peter and Paul perform together since Mary had passed away. I went to the show, and Noel (Paul) invited me for drinks back at his hotel after the concert. Over cocktails, he talked about how much he had liked my last album, *Awakenings*. He had an idea of me performing songs from that album wearing blue jeans and a flannel shirt. While I played the dulcimer, a tall, beautiful woman in an evening gown stood behind me, playing a synthesizer. It was an interesting idea, but I just brushed it off as backstage chatter and didn't think to pursue it any further.

A few weeks went by. One night, while I sat on my couch listening to a Peter, Paul & Mary song on the internet, the phone rang. It was Noel. "Your songs are too good to just put out on a random CD." He wanted me to record a new album for his label with some of the songs from *Awakenings* and some new ones he wanted me to write. His idea was that I would record my dulcimer and vocal tracks, and then his friend, Michael McInnis, who played the synthesizer, would write and play arrangements for each song. He promised me that he would help me find an agent and get the word out so I could get booked, earn a living, and sell the recording. Stunned and honored that my mentor was offering me a record deal on his own label, I began to think maybe, just maybe, this was the beginning: my adult music career was on its way back.

This was just after I had my Moh's surgery on my nose. While healing and hiding in my apartment with bandages wrapped across my face, I began to read some of Yogananda and Ramana Maharshi's books, so I was in the spiritual flow. My friend Jerry Rockwell made a beautiful new dulcimer for me as a gift, and it was perfect to use for creating new songs. Each new song that I wrote and sent to Noel, he loved. Often, he made slight adjustments to the lyrics. As soon as all the songs were complete, I was in the recording studio, making the new album.

It was a few months after I finished my part of the record that I was scheduled for some tests to see if a small lump under my chin was cancerous or not. After the results came back, I called Noel. I told him that I had just been diagnosed with stage 3 melanoma and given a fatal prognosis. "So, it looks like my music career started with you and is going to end with you, as well."

"If anyone can beat melanoma, it's you, and I have no doubt you'll get through it with flying colors."

Seven years later while we were having lunch, I asked him how he had known I would be fine. "I was just being encouraging," he said, but I think he had a premonition.

The new album, *Reawakening,* was released on Noel's label, New World, a few months later. It was a really different recording for me; I had never before recorded with just a synthesizer for my entire "band," and I didn't know Michael, so I had relied on Noel's suggestions and the tracks that were sent to me by email. When the album came out, it received good reviews and was nominated for an award in Europe. Although Noel had tried to find an agent for me, no one was interested. The music business was still stuck in the mud for many musicians, regardless of genre, due to the economy. But the album gave me hope, a direction to follow, and I had nothing to lose.

A few months after *Reawakening* was released, I began to plan a move back to San Diego. I couldn't really afford to live in California, but I also knew that I couldn't afford to stay in Kansas for more important reasons than money. Fortunately, I had the will power to do whatever it took to change my life and be happier, so I created a new story for myself and started to figure out how it would all come together. In May 2016, I packed up the jeep again and headed farther west with Bosco for one of the most mystical three-day drives of my life.

***

Originally, I wrote the song, "Dorothy," which appears on *Reawakening,* with Noel. A year or so later, I added a verse about going to California, which I released on *The Deviant Dulcimerist* and which appears on the album accompanying this book.

Dorothy

I told a friend I was moving to Kansas
He said, what kind of person decides to move there?
I said, I've got a feeling it will be a respite
So, I'm packing up my Toto and all my affairs
I said, I've got a feeling all kinds of things
Are gonna turn around and come around
and be what I need
Just like Dorothy landing in Oz

AWAKENING, COINCIDENCES, AND SYNCHRONICITY

Riding the tornado into make-believe

Dorothy, are you there? I could use some company
Don't forget to leave those ruby slippers for me
I need a fast track for making my way back
From the lion and the scarecrow and the tin man

It all turned into quite a cosmic Kansas
Who would have guessed, who could have known?
No one would believe this crazy life I'm living
Between the yellow brick road and the twilight zone

Don't mind the man behind the curtain
Smoke and mirror is his game
Take the time to find the answer
Isn't that the reason that you came?

So, I packed my bags and headed back to California
You know there really is no place like home
You've got to have the brains, the courage, and the heart
To follow your rainbow wherever you roam

Words by Kevin Roth & Noel Paul Stookey.
Music by Kevin Roth.

Chapter 6
The Incredible Lightness of Being—Kansas to California

"Toto, I don't think we're in Kansas anymore."
—The Wizard of Oz

With Bosco curled up in his dog bed on the passenger seat and the back of my Jeep full of dulcimers, paintings, and clothes, I began a three-day drive from Kansas to San Diego. GPS had me driving through Kansas, Colorado, and Arizona, and then into California. I had found an apartment in San Diego a few months earlier online and had arranged for a bed to be delivered on the evening of my arrival. I also secured a temporary part-time job so I could pay some bills until I figured out what was next for my life.

When I started driving west, I felt excited and numb at the same time. Who wouldn't after what I had been through? The decision to move to San Diego felt like one of the best decisions of my life. It had perfect weather, a relaxed scene, and was much more liberal than Kansas. Bosco would also be much happier there because he hated snow and rain, and there was neither in San Diego unless you drove to the mountains.

Life Review

My first day on the road felt like a life review. I thought about everything I had been through during my lifetime. I shook my head at all the things I had accomplished and survived. I didn't know whether to feel sorry for myself or blessed. I settled for a little of both. During my stay in Kansas, I had become quite a different man. I had found the teachings on self-realization. It was the beginning of a new spiritual wisdom that was wonderful, interesting, and finally gave me a sense of peace. There was still a chance the melanoma would return at some point, but for now, the coast was clear. Cancer had presented the opportunity to get clear on exactly what I didn't want in my life any longer: stress, negativity, drama, financial concerns, and being thirty pounds overweight.

On the second day, I entered Colorado and thought about what I wanted my future life to really look and feel like. I remembered the OBE vision I had when I was eight, a premonition of the three different phases my life would go through. Instinctively, I knew I was entering the third and final phase.

Time-Lapse

Driving into Arizona, I noticed how dry everything looked compared to the mountains of Colorado, the incredible views and lush colors. I was daydreaming about my future life in California when I experienced what almost seemed like a lapse in time. I was driving through the desert, and I picked up a radio station playing American Indian flute music that was incredibly beautiful. In between the flute and chanting were spoken meditations about one's spiritual life and direction. Kismet? I lost all sense of time while driving and listening to the mystical music. It had happened just as I began to imagine my future. After what seemed hours, the station disappeared. I tried turning the radio dial to see if I could tune into it again, but it was gone. The experience was so lovely that I later bought some Native American Indian flutes to try to capture the sound and feeling, but nothing could compare to the experience I had on that day.

Unconditional Love

As I was driving out of the desert and into the first metropolitan area that I had seen for quite a while, a terrible windstorm kicked up. Tractor trailers swayed, and I got nervous about driving. It takes a lot to freak me out, since I had driven thousands of miles on concert tours during my life. I thought I'd better pull off into a hotel and wait this one out. I found one a few miles down the road. When I looked over at Bosco, something suddenly changed inside me. He was curled up in his bed, sleeping, and I suddenly realized how lucky I was to have a fur angel I could count on for friendship, companionship, fun, wet kisses, a wagging tail, and pure unadulterated, unconditional love any time of the day or night. He was my buddy, my pal, my road warrior. He completely melted my heart.

After I checked into the hotel, I realized they didn't allow pets. I put Bosco in a big backpack and sneaked him into the side entrance close to my room. I ordered a pizza, and after sharing it with Bosco, I took a bath and watched TV until we both fell asleep on the lumpy king-size mattress. In the morning, I went down to the lobby where they were serving breakfast and got two big plates full of bacon and eggs, Bosco's favorite! After a walk and one more cup of coffee for the road, we headed towards California with the sun shining and Joni Mitchell on the stereo singing, "I am on a lonely road and I am traveling, traveling, traveling. Looking for something, what can it be?"

San Diego, Here We Come!

The next day, the long drive to California seemed to drag on. I was anxious to get to my new apartment before the bed was delivered early that evening. As I saw the highway sign that read San Diego, I began to feel excited and hopeful. It had been at least fifteen years since I had lived there, but I still remembered the beautiful beaches and laid-back vibe. I was looking forward to getting reacquainted with the city.

I walked into my new apartment, set down a small grocery bag of food, unleashed Bosco, and watched him sniff the joint out. I leaned against a sunny wall and felt a sigh of relief. I heard a dog bark in the distance as the cars drove past my window. It all seemed surreal. There's something about seeing four blank, white walls in a brand-new empty apartment that invites renewal, hope, new beginnings, and possibilities. I was home, finally. No more

Florida, no more Kansas, no more Kevin Roth the entertainer. Just me, my dachshund, and some dulcimers. I sat down on the carpet, unwrapped my tuna sandwich, and shared it with Bosco as we waited for the bed to be delivered. I couldn't have been happier.

Unexpected Possibilities

The first year in San Diego was life-changing. I started to write songs for a new album called *The Deviant Dulcimerist,* which was a musical portrait of my life in California. It's a fun, sweet, and quirky album. I had a blast creating the music and cover artwork of me as a bohemian playing the dulcimer, with Bosco playing the bongos. To this day, it's one of my favorite albums. I was loving music and being creative again. Money was still tight, but I was happy, healthy, and I loved being back in California. I started hiking, taking Bosco to the beach, and slowly making new friends.

After the album came out, a friend asked me what project I was going to work on next. I told him I'd probably write another album and see if I could get a small tour going. He gave me a meaningful look. "You just came through a life-changing experience. Why don't you teach others how to get through their stress, and help them find more joy and fun in life like you did? Become a life coach!"

I had no idea what he meant. I'd never heard of a life coach before. I googled it and told him I didn't think that was my cup of tea, but the more I thought about it, the more my gut was telling me I might just be good at that sort of thing and to pursue it.

One day I was talking to a professional life coach about the ins and outs of the business, and I mentioned that I'd have to sideline the music until a life coaching business had been established, due to the amount of work it would take to set up the business. He looked at me and smiled. He said, "Kevin, when you play the dulcimer, it's incredibly meditative. Use the dulcimer with your coaching. It's like *Dulcimeditation.* A bell went off in my head.

I began to think about the steps I took that got me through the difficult times. I wrote out exactly what I had done that moved me past stinkin' thinkin' to having a vision for my life that was full of hope, fun, and success. But looking at the cost of getting a new business off the ground, with advertising and other expenses, I realized I didn't have the money to pull it off. Then Covid happened, and the entire world shut down.

As worried as I was about catching Covid, I also saw it as an opportunity to get my new business idea going, because in California, the state was paying people's health insurance, giving them unemployment and extra money to live on, and even paid the rent for eighteen months. I was literally given a free opportunity to put my life coaching ideas together without worrying about money to see if it would work. The entire world was quarantined, so I had all the time in the world.

Once I got a feeling for how I could help others, I mentioned my idea of Dulcimeditation in Facebook dulcimer groups. I told them how I could help with stress and bring more joy into people's lives. Talk about timing: everyone was stressed to the max except me. I was healthy, I kept to myself, I didn't have to worry about money, and I could start a new business that interested me.

I started working with two clients who were dulcimer players. I had no idea if what I planned to teach them would work, but I was amazed and delighted that their lives improved within the first few sessions. I knew in my gut that I had a rhythm for this type of work, so I continued teaching others, but I dropped the term "life coach" and called myself a "creative life designer," because I had literally redesigned a new vision of my life back in Kansas. I knew exactly what I had done to change my attitude and diet and the techniques I had used effectively to heal my life. I began to teach this to others, and my business began to take off. I was amazed at my success.

For people who didn't play the dulcimer, I played it for them during the beginning of our sessions as a relaxation technique. Just as I had caught the dulcimer and the children's music wave, I caught a new wave and created my own niche. I established the term Dulcimeditation around the internet, recorded an album with Dulcimeditation music, and even designed a dulcimer that people could purchase, *The Wink Cosmic Dulcimer.*

During my own journey I discovered that knowing what mattered, why it mattered, and having a game plan was great, but it wasn't enough. I had to figure out how to control my monkey mind daily, so when my life felt out of balance, I could use certain techniques to quiet my mind and rebalance. Discovering these techniques and how to use them, which I cover later in this book, was the glue that held everything together for me. When I use mindful awareness along with these revelations, I not only know how to ride the waves in life but I also enjoy the ride.

In hindsight, I can see that all my life experiences have led me to this point. This, my third phase of life as foretold in my precognitive and OBE experiences, is expanding beyond my wildest dreams.

***

The Incredible Lightness of Being

He headed west with nothing left
Just a broken dream and a new beginning
He turned his headlights low as it began to snow
Sometimes you have to just drive
right into your own sweet sunset
A second chance, again, to let it all go

Oh, the incredible lightness of being

Colorado, Arizona, California, one long highway
Life's a byway, really, one long song
He drove for hours steeped in silence
Only heard the hum of eighteen wheelers
Riding into the night and the light of dawn

Oh, the incredible lightness of being

It doesn't matter where you've been
Doesn't matter where you're going
Life's for knowing what will be is gonna be
He used to have a lot of expectations
Now it comes down to the realization
That it's only love that will set him free

Oh, the incredible lightness of being

He moved into his new apartment
Four white walls and a big wide window
He closed his eyes and leaned against the sunny wall
He heard a dog bark in the distance
While the cars rushed past his window
Everybody's in a hurry, going nowhere at all

Oh, the incredible lightness of being

Words and music by Kevin Roth.

Section 2

EPIPHANIES AND AHA! MOMENTS

Chapter 7
Discovering Your Path
—The Inside Job

"The next message you need is
always right where you are."
—Ram Dass

In 2001, I was on a concert tour with my accompanist, Mitchell Schecter. We were playing a string of one-night stands across the country. When we pulled up to The Strand Theater in Oconomowoc, Wisconsin, I saw my name on the movie marquee. I was elated. My favorite movie, *The Wizard of Oz,* had its premiere at The Strand on August 12, 1939. It wasn't in Hollywood or New York; but in Wisconsin, on the very stage where I would sing that evening. It was my premier there, singing and playing the dulcimer and piano. Inside the lobby, I took in movie history. There were old photographs from the movie premiere and a photo of the marquee on which my name now appeared: THE WIZARD OF OZ. What a blast. It was an old, beautifully preserved theater, historic.

As I was getting ready to go on stage, the theater director came into my dressing room wearing a smile as wide as a four-lane highway. "The Red Hat Society is here!" he announced. I turned to Mitchell as if he might know who the hell The Red Hat Society was, which, of course, he didn't. As it turned out, there are groups of women across the country who are members of a social club called The Red Hat Society, whose specific dress code included, obviously, red hats. I assumed by the promoter's exuberance that this group was a big deal, which meant the show had to be amazing. I was super excited to play there, and we were on fire that night. We closed the show with an encore of *Over the Rainbow*. After the show, I went out to the lobby to greet the ladies in red and answered the usual questions about the tour, where I lived, how long I had been playing the dulcimer, and so on.

Back at my hotel after the concert, I was enveloped by a sense of falling into an abyss of emptiness, uncertainty, and longing. I was all too familiar with those dull aching feelings from many years of being a vagabond and chasing a musical career. Nothing seemed to make sense. The concert had gone well, I sold a ton of recordings, and yet there I sat, staring at myself in the hotel mirror, depressed and confused. It took me years to realize what had happened: I still believed that fame and fortune would bring me happiness.

The subtle aching loneliness I felt on and off the road had nothing to do with being single. It came from a longing for a deep connection with something I could never quite put my finger on. It was so damn frustrating! I sensed a nebulous calling inside my soul, as if someone were whispering in my ear, "Turn around." And when I did, no one was there. This subtle inner voice had always been there, waiting, watching, and whispering, "Come back home." But where was home?

Even as a young child, this world never felt like home, and it never made any sense. It didn't matter how many friends and lovers I had or how many marquees displayed my name; there was a hole in me that no one and nothing could fill. Since it seemed impossible to find an answer inside myself, I began to search outside and discovered the world of self-help books, self-professed enlightened beings, and gurus in business suits who were more than willing to sell me the TRUTH. Like an addict, I became a self-help junkie.

A friend once joked that he was going to write a self-help book for me, called, *How to Stop Buying Self-Help Books!* In my search, I became hooked on new-age, woo-woo teachers who told me they knew exactly what I needed to do, how I needed to think, and which affirmations I needed to say to find inner peace. I bought the books, meditations, and courses, but they always were only a temporary fix for feeling whole. Every book, lecture, and self-help guru I came across presented a new twist, and each time I was sure that, finally, this time, I would be "fixed" for good, but it never lasted. And so, on to the next self-help book.

I even sang in many churches and fellowships that preached inner peace and abundance. At one of the churches where I sang occasionally, the reverend told me they were cutting the performer fees because the budget was too tight. "I don't understand; you teach abundance but are always struggling financially. Why?" Need I say I was never invited back there to sing?

What ended my addiction to self-help books, pity parties, and feeling helpless was getting the prognosis of a death sentence. BOOM! No more affirmations for me. I got up off my ass and did something about my life. The first thing I did was curse God out—literally. After all the financial crap I went through, the stuttering of my career, the death of my father, and other smaller disasters, I stood in my apartment and screamed at God in rage. "How *dare* you give me cancer! Screw this. Take me now, because I'm finished with your holy bull and all your spiritual crap. I'm done!"

I guess he/she heard me, because everything started to change after my little tantrum. In my defense, back in Florida, I had asked "the universe" for spiritual enlightenment. Melanoma did the trick, for sure. Be assured that with any future Godly requests I make, I will attach an addendum stating the way I'd like it to go.

Books That Mattered

I switched from devouring self-help books by the dozen to relying on a few spiritual books that gave me tremendous hope and put me on a path I felt in my gut was what I needed to get the job done. These spiritual books focused on non-duality, self-realization, the mystical teachings of Christ, Ramana Maharshi, and later, books by Robert Wolfe about *Ajata*.

The Spiritual Path Is a Slow-Drip Process

I'm not knocking all self-help books, including this one. However, I have discovered that most good books and retreats are simply pointers. No matter how many books I've read, spiritual retreats I've attended, or gurus I've gathered, the one thing I've come to understand is this: the spiritual path is an inside job. It's a gradual process. I have found that it works best to analyze the information I gather and allow understanding to unfold within me over time so that it becomes a part of me.

For example, I am always amazed that I can repeatedly read the same paragraph of a meaningful book, and each time, the meaning deepens. That's why I call this the slow-drip process towards understanding who you are. There are days when I am drawn to study a tremendous number of concepts and lessons and other days when I just can't read one more word. Such feelings are normal parts of the journey. They allow enough time to breathe and process the information I've taken in.

Self-Kindness and Self-Compassion Were Crucial

Being kind and patient with myself was key. If God or consciousness is supposed to be all-forgiving, then there's no reason why I can't give myself a break and not take it all so seriously.

I Had to Walk the Talk

It's important to act according to what I know, to "walk the talk" as I understand it and to stick with what works. Once

I resonated with a concept, I applied it to my life. When I experienced that sitting quietly and listening within for guidance helped my life, I realized I needed to practice it. I share this with my students and clients, who say they find this more like a behavioral change than a practice because they quickly learn that when they walk the talk, that is, when they actually make these changes they've learned about, their lives improve quickly.

I don't think of this as "practice makes perfect." Why? Because the spiritual path is never perfect. It evolves. Only the One reality exists as perfection.

To simplify things, here is what I recommend: In your explorations, find what works for you and begin to apply it in your life as best you can.

I found it was easy for me to think that all I needed to do was show up at a retreat or listen to a video of a spiritual teacher, and I'd have all I needed. But as one of my teachers said, "You need to not just understand or be aware of it, you need to know it, which comes from investigating it within yourself."

This spiritual path is not about graduating with a higher-learning degree. What I've experienced for myself is this: as more things become clear, such as my desires and attachments, eventually they are no longer needed and are shed like the skin of a snake. Life becomes simple and clear. I also don't kid myself; I may feel I'm riding a spiritual high for a while, but I always know that expansion and contraction are constantly in motion, so I never assume my lessons are learned and finished with.

I recently found a photograph taken of me on stage at The Strand Theater. Just like Dorothy, I thought to myself, the road I'm traveling is long and there are plenty of lessons to learn about my heart, my brain, and courage. Through Red Hats and yellow brick roads, it all turned out right in the end. My journey has required balance, surrender, determination, and investigation, but I have arrived to where I needed to be and I have kept going. I still have a song in my heart and a sneaky grin on my face, thinking about how Dorothy and I had our premiers in the same place and, in a way, reached a similar conclusion.

***

The Inside Job

There're so many things I don't understand
Like the Universe within as black holes expand
The subconscious mind of the half-conscious man
It's all an inside job

Some say the end of time is near
Others claim it's already here
One minute comes as the last disappears
It's all an inside job

There's a cosmic order to this happenstance
A delicate balance to this romance
Like fractals expanding in an infinite dance

It's all an inside job

We long for love, so many strive
To understand the meaning of their lives
In the end, what's on that other side?
It's all an inside job

Meanings change as you grow
What I knew for sure now isn't quite so
Here's to illusions that we've come to know
It's all an inside job

Words and music by Kevin Roth.

Chapter 8
Universal Awareness
—The Urge to Merge

"You are that One reality that never comes or goes."
—Author Unknown

When we are born, we are connected to the subtle awareness of infinite love and wholeness. As we grow older, this awareness fades into the background as our ego/mind develops and we go about living our lives. And yet, this subtle feeling continues to whisper within us, waiting to be heard. People who have spoken of near-death experiences claim that when they clinically died, they felt themselves leaving their bodies and experienced a sensation of wholeness and love. They experienced a recognizable sense of knowing "everything" that exists, which was beyond any feelings or thoughts they had ever experienced or imagined. These experiencers describe being in a place they almost invariably call *home*.

Whether we are aware of it or not, we all share a longing to reconnect to this sense of *home* while still living our lives. We are searching for that wholeness of being connected to the infinite One reality. The truth is, we have never been disconnected. The urge to merge with this One reality is most natural and is the easiest thing to do because it already is who we are. We are what we are seeking; we just need to recognize it.

Throughout our lives, our desires and attachments veil this truth and temporarily satisfy the longing. We are like fish in the ocean of maya (illusion), looking for water. This is so simple that it's almost incomprehensible because the mind likes to complicate things.

Having faith, certitude, and determination was paramount for my journey. I'm not talking about blind faith, but about trusting my gut. I learned that my intuition, my inner voice, is, in fact, the One reality guiding me. I have an acronym for faith:

Following

An

Intuition

That

Helps

As I teach my students, when you replace what doesn't work in your life with what does, you never go back. An example is when my gut told me to drop the victim story I had created for myself in Kansas and create a beautiful new story of success and happiness in its place. When I moved to California, I had faith in my intention to live my last few years in a free, easy, and happy lifestyle. Feeling like a victim and feeling like a victor were as different to me as night and day. Obviously, I didn't die, so I continue to live this way.

Here's my bottom line: Just as music comes to me naturally, or just as an artist who has never had an art lesson can paint a portrait, I'm pretty convinced that my "doing" is not entirely "me" doing it. So, what is? I'll never know what "It" is. It's impossible to identify or wrap your mind around what God or Consciousness is because, as the ancient spiritual texts and even part of science will tell you, *It* is formless and empty. As the Buddhist heart sutra says, "Form is emptiness, and emptiness is form." Both Bob Dylan and Leonard Cohen, two of the greatest songwriters of our time, have said that they don't write the songs; what does write them is a mystery.

When a song comes to me, I feel a subtle nudging to sit down with my dulcimer or piano and channel a musical and lyrical dictation of what is coming through. Many artists and musicians call this "channeling the muse." Often, some lyrics will come that I must look up in a dictionary because I'm not quite sure what they mean, and I am always astonished to find that they make perfect sense. I'm not a disciplined writer. I only write when I feel something needs to be said. I cannot call on the muse to show up and write a song or a book at my beck and call. How any of this works is a total enigma. The one thing I am sure of is this: as this planet spins approximately one thousand miles an hour and hangs in the infinite vastness of what science calls dark matter, the idea that I am entirely in charge of what happens in my life is ridiculous.

***

One

There is something I must tell you,
I've waited far too long
I hope you listen closely,
and you won't take this wrong
You've been asking everybody
what to do and where to go
When the answer to your questions
you already know

You can blame your life on everyone
or the zodiac and stars
It doesn't matter what you do
or who you think you are
Somewhere in your heart you know
you're more than what you see
And you can step beyond the limits of reality

And it's all just one, and it's everything
And no one knows where it ends or begins
And we're made of stars and when we die
We will leave this world and be sanctified

You can laugh away your sorrows;
you can think that money buys

UNIVERSAL AWARENESS—THE URGE TO MERGE

Everything you've ever wanted,
until it opens your eyes
That longing in your heart cries out
but the calling never dies
Everything is waiting for you when you realize

I'm here to tell you it's not all what it seems
Got to row your boat ashore cause life is but a dream
Time to wake up to the calling if you listen you will hear
Some days it seems to fade away,
but it never disappears

Words and music by Kevin Roth.

Chapter 9
The Illusion
—Is Any of This Real?

"The more we delve into quantum mechanics the stranger the world becomes."
—Kevin Michael

One summer, as I was body surfing in the ocean, I turned around and saw an enormous wave coming towards me. There was no way to dive into it or outrun it. I knew I was going to get hit hard, and there was nothing I could do about it. I remember the roar and watching it grow into a monster barreling towards me. Within a few seconds, I was tossed like a rag doll in turbulent, murky green, sandy water. I was petrified. When it hit, I heard a voice inside me say, "Let go, relax, and it will be okay. Don't fight it." The wave spit me out on the beach, and when I got up, covered in sand, I saw a couple standing near me. Their mouths were open and they were shaking their heads as if to say, "Man, you're one lucky dude!" They told me they watched the wave swallow me. Can you imagine? I'm sure if I had fought the wave, it easily could have broken my back.

I've had similar occurrences throughout my life. One of the most bizarre happened while I was driving on the turnpike. Out of the blue, not even fifteen minutes away from my exit, I had an urge to pull off into a restaurant at a rest stop on the turnpike. I wasn't hungry, I didn't need gas, and I knew there were plenty of restaurants just off my exit, so there was no logical explanation for deciding to stop there. After I had finished a cup of coffee, I heard a trucker say that there had been a massive pile-up on the turnpike right before my exit, and there had been casualties. Instinctively, I knew I would have been part of that pile-up if I hadn't pulled off.

When I think about all the precognitive experiences I've had, the inner voices and feelings I've paid attention to, and the "knowledge" that I would *not* die of melanoma even when oncologists said I would, I can't help thinking that this world is one strange place, and what I think is going on ain't all there is!

These strange, unexplainable occurrences happen to millions of other people. Often, they are afraid to talk about what occurred because they can find no logical explanation for it and they're afraid they'll be called crazy. Moreover, people want to feel that they're in control of their lives, so when something odd occurs, they may feel that their relative world has somehow changed, and they don't know how to process it. Many people, including me, have never spoken about having had an out-of-body or near-death experience until they discovered that other people have had similar experiences and feel comfortable sharing.

Before I investigated science, near-death experiences, the mystical teachings of Christ, and other spiritual materials, the relative world seemed like the only reality, and the woo-woo world made no logical sense. Now, the reverse seems true for me. According to science, everyone's possessions and, in fact, everything in this vast universe consists of 99.9999999 percent empty space. That being true, are *we* empty? Do I even exist? The universe keeps expanding, but into what? So, what *is* real? As my friend and author Robert Wolfe explained:

> What is real must be always real, not a condition
> which can die, or has died. What has had neither
> a beginning nor an ending cannot die. Where that
> which has neither beginning nor ending is the
> real reality, what does that tell us about the
> world, our mind, and senses, and indeed us?

At first, this line of thought seemed confusing, but I found over time that it made perfect sense. Adopting this new view of reality took the heaviness out of everything I considered a significant event in my life. Things I once thought incredibly important and took seriously were just blips on a screen. My life changed. I changed. Instead of feeling conflicted and oh-so-serious, I was having more fun and feeling animated.

At the Institute of Noetic Sciences, visionary leaders in the fields of consciousness, transformation, healthcare, and cutting-edge science gather scientists and sages to explore how parts of science now agree with what ancient spiritual texts have said on the topics of reality and illusion. I find this fascinating and impossible to ignore. Dr. Eben Alexander, a neurosurgeon, and Dr. Mary Neal, a spinal surgeon, are just two of the thousands who have had NDE experiences and who report that this world is not at all what we think it is. I read an article in *Esquire Magazine* years ago about the renowned movie critic Roger Ebert. His wife, Chaz Ebert, spoke about Roger's experience shortly before he passed away:

> The day before he passed away, [Roger] wrote
> me a note: "This is all an elaborate hoax." I asked
> him, "What's a hoax?" And he was talking about
> this world, this place. He said it was an illusion.
> He described it as a vastness that you can't even
> imagine. It was a place where the past, present,
> and future were happening all at once.[1]

After sifting through religious, spiritual, and scientific information and reflecting on my personal experience, I finally discovered what I believe is the answer that ties everything together for me. *Ajata*. Ramana Maharshi best explains it:

> There is no doubt whatsoever that the universe is
> the merest illusion. Clearly perceive, beyond all
> doubt, that the phenomenal world (as an
> objective, independent reality) is wholly non-
> existent. There is no creation, no destruction, no
> bondage, no longing to be freed from bondage,

---

[1] https://www.esquire.com/entertainment/tv/news/a26606/roger-ebert-final-moments/

no striving to be free (from bondage), nor anyone who has attained (freedom from bondage). Know that this is the ultimate truth.

I'll be the first to say that this seems to make no logical sense in our relative world. When you fall in love, you just know it. When I first heard the dulcimer, I knew it was my destiny. The same feeling happened to me when I learned about *Ajata*, which explains that the phenomenal world does not actually exist. Even as a young man, I sensed this ultimate truth. If you'd like a deeper understanding of *Ajata*, I highly recommend Robert Wolfe's website: AjataSunyata.com.

As I integrated this information into my life, I began to think and live differently. I no longer get stressed out. I do what I need to do to pay bills, stay healthy, and be happy. On the rare occasion I become unhappy, I realize it's my ego/mind, and that, too, is an illusion. This being so, why bother getting upset when someone tells me I'm crazy or that things don't work out the way my ego wants them to?

To be honest, life has become quite entertaining. I laugh at many things as if they're a cosmic joke. It's like living in The Twilight Zone and The Matrix simultaneously.

Suggested Readings
- *Emptiness,* by Robert Wolfe
- *Happiness and the Art of Being,* by Michael James

Both authors have written extensively on the subject of *Ajata*.

***

Adrift

We come spinning out of nothingness,
scattering stars like dust
We're just waves of possibilities,
there really is no us
There is no time, there is no place,
it's only just a dream
There really is no birth or death
and nothing in-between

I asked him, "How can you explain
this life to me?"
He said it all exists as a dream,
my friend, within relativity
It's a picture show on a cosmic screen
perceived through your eye
The only question to ask yourself really is,
who am I?

Some say that the world began with
the Big Bang long ago
But what created the cosmic bang,
no one seems to know
No words can explain the Infinite,
yet silence speaks to me

THE ILLUSION—IS ANY OF THIS REAL?

So, let come what comes,
let go what goes,
adrift in the cosmic sea

Words and music by Kevin Roth.

Chapter 10
Everyday Joy—Tacos and the Quiet Times

"They say a person needs just three things to find joy in this world: someone to love, something to do, and something to look forward to."
—As told to Kevin Roth by Bud Reed/Tom Bodett

One of many lessons I learned about joy and the simple pleasures of life was served up to me at a taco stand on my sixtieth birthday. That day at the stand, I noticed two Mexican migrant workers who were sitting at a table eating tacos and drinking Coronas. They were laughing as if they had just won the lottery. On the other side of the table a businessman paced back and forth, a taco in one hand and a cellphone in the other, yelling at someone on the phone about a money issue. Red taco sauce ran down the side of his hand as I watched. At first, I thought it was blood, but it was just an interesting metaphor. The guy obviously had more money than the two migrant workers; yet he looked miserable.

Most people I know with a lot of money or fame never seem as content or as down-to-earth as those who have much less to live on. The universe gave me a tremendous birthday gift that day. It reminded me how wealthy I was to have a few good friends, a pooch I loved, and the blessing to be a successful artist, musician, and teacher, who, in my own way, makes the world a more interesting and happier place.

Another huge lesson on simple everyday joys occurred when I was fifteen. As a young folk singer, I befriended an older woman who played the clawhammer banjo and sang. Her name was Ola Belle Reed. She called herself a proud hillbilly, and she was. Ola Belle was well known in folk and country music circles as a musician, but more important, she was adored for the way she treated other people. She saw everyone as a precious human being who just wanted to be loved. Everyone who met Ola Belle loved her.

Ola Belle taught me about the art of joy and contentment. No matter how down I felt when I went to see her, she always picked me up by reminding me to stay positive, happy, and grateful for my "God-given musical gifts in life." She believed that everyday joy can be found in nature, a smile, simple kindness, and just knowing you are loved. "Think good thoughts, and good things will happen." Her love and her optimism made it impossible to be depressed around her.

Ola Belle's little house on Principio Road was a community gathering spot, full of music, food, and good times. There was always cornbread in the oven, pinto beans on the stove, and sweet tea in the refrigerator for all the friends and family members who stopped by daily to chat with her and to pick a tune with her and her son David and husband Bud. I spent many nights on her couch underneath homemade quilts, falling asleep to the sound of her softly picking the banjo.

One day, we were standing underneath a big tree in her yard when she pointed to the leaves and said, "Look, it's gonna rain. When the leaves are turned upwards like that, it's a sign there's a storm coming." When I looked up at the sky, all I saw were a few scattered clouds. As I looked at her with doubt written all over my face, she took me by the hand, looked me straight in the eye, and quoted from the Bible, "Be still and know that I am God," then added, "There are things in life, mysteries we don't know about that nature can teach us." Within an hour, it poured rain. That memory has stayed with me ever since.

From the first time we met, we formed a deep connection. I kiddingly called her my guru, but I really thought of her as my second mother. The feeling was mutual, because she referred to me as her number-three son. She was an angel whom I deeply needed and deeply miss.

Over the years since she's been gone, I had forgotten the lessons she taught me about the simple gifts in life that bring you joy, but I remembered them when I moved back to California and found old photographs of us together. Looking at them, I realized that having a mentor and friend like Ola Belle was another beautiful gift in my life. Her wisdom and spiritual guidance inspired the song "The Quiet Times."

***

The Quiet Times

Take your troubles and your pain,
all your worries and your blame
Take your life that's torn apart
and come with me
To a place I've come to know
in times like these I go
Inside of the quiet times again

Lullaby your cares away,
think good thoughts
and good things will happen
Rest your mind and things will pass in time,
I know they will
There's magic in the quiet times they say

The old folks from the hills lived a life
of peace and fortune
Not for money or for riches did they care
But for love, good crops, and a blue sky,
with a prayer of thanks and blessings
Far richer for the quiet times they shared

Take a lesson from this world,
it's a world too fast for dreamers
Still, there's one thing a man can never change

EVERYDAY JOY—TACOS AND THE QUIET TIMES

Like the blowing of the wind,
or the laughter of the children
And knowing there's a quiet time
to find your soul again

Words and music by Kevin Roth.

Chapter 11
Music Healing—The Power of Dulcimeditation

"There ain't no notes on the dulcimer, you just play it."
—Unknown

The mountain dulcimer is an American folk instrument with a history that goes as far back as the early 1800s, originating in the Appalachian Mountains. It is a type of fretted lap zither that is related to the French Epinette, Norwegian Langeleik, Swedish Hummel, and German Scheitholt.

When most people hear a dulcimer for the first time, it is usually being played in a simple, traditional folk style. Folk singers like Jean Ritchie, John Jacob Niles, and other traditional players popularized the dulcimer in the early 1960s, during the early folk music boom. In the late '60s and early '70s, more contemporary players like Richard Fariña and Joni Mitchell further popularized the dulcimer in the singer-songwriter genre.

I first heard the dulcimer played by Anne Stokes in 1972 at a meditation gathering near Philadelphia, Pennsylvania. I was fourteen years old. I went to the gathering not because

I was interested in meditation but because I had been introduced to a fellow musician, Chuck Rabb, who knew Anne and claimed she sang like Joni Mitchell. I was a huge Joni Mitchell fan, so I tagged along for the evening. Anne was sitting in the kitchen playing her dulcimer and singing a song called "Simple Gifts." From the moment I heard the dulcimer, I was hooked.

Not long after, my high school music teacher informed me that there was a dulcimer for sale at a nearby bookstore, The Decoy Book Shop. I immediately went in and bought it for around one hundred dollars. Anne was kind enough to come to where I lived and show me a little bit about how to play it. I never took lessons, read an instruction book, or even discovered other dulcimer players in my area for quite some time. I wasn't even aware that Joni Mitchell had just recorded her now classic album, *Blue*, which featured four dulcimer songs. I took my musical ear along with my piano experience and created the sound I wanted on the dulcimer, thinking of it as a blank musical canvas on which to create. Because I was used to playing the piano in a downward hand position, playing the dulcimer on my lap seemed much easier than learning the guitar. It was certainly more portable than a piano. Quite simply, the dulcimer captured my heart.

I didn't know many traditional folk songs at the time and wasn't even aware there was a particular way or style of playing the dulcimer, so any song I played on the piano, such as "Over the Rainbow," or simply composed was just a given. At the beginning of my career, the traditional dulcimer folk police were aghast when I stepped out of the traditional "dulcimore" style and performed original songs or Bob Marley songs on their American folk instrument. Interestingly enough, it was my innovative approach that got me to sign my first recording contract with Folkways records in 1974. The timing was perfect: it was the beginning of the dulcimer boom of the early 70s. Because my recordings were among a handful of albums to be found featuring the dulcimer, and because my style was contemporary and innovative, I quickly became known in the dulcimer world. I suppose one could call it all kismet.

Looking back, I realize that the dulcimer has always been an unusual musical lifeboat for me. Even my introduction through Anne was unique. When I met her, she was moving away from being a folk singer after she had met a Sufi Sheikh named Bawa Muhaiyaddeen and became dedicated to his teachings. Because Anne and I had a connection, I followed her to the Bawa Muhaiyaddeen Fellowship. That was the beginning of my "formal" spiritual journey. Almost forty-five years later, I described to someone what happens when I play: "When I am playing, sometimes I space out and lose all track of time."

"Oh, so it's like Dulcimeditation," he said. That was when I realized that, for years, I had been doing my own type of musical meditation while at the same time listening to guidance from my inner voice.

When I thought about getting into coaching and teaching, I was not planning to include the dulcimer. However, my friend advised that I teach Dulcimeditation to both dulcimer players and others who came to me, as it was a unique approach to well-being. The dulcimer is also an amazingly easy instrument to learn, and the Dulcimeditation playing style is extremely simple. I've taught it to musicians, but also to many who had always wanted to play an instrument but never thought they could. That's the powerful thing about the dulcimer and Dulcimeditation; anyone can benefit from its beauty.

Later, I used my friend Robert Worth's cosmic sound hole design of the stars, moon, and sun and asked The Dulcimer Shoppe to build what I call a "Cosmic Wink" dulcimer. The name is based on the idea of chilling out and napping. The cosmic planetary sound hole design represents a fun spiritual and meditative concept. I have since created several recordings of Dulcimeditation and I sell Cosmic Wink dulcimers on my website to folks worldwide. Each customer's dulcimer is custom-built and is offered with Dulcimeditation lessons. The woods are chosen especially for a meditative, sweet, and mellow sound.

Dulcimeditation is played in a relaxed, easy fashion. I never play any song the same way twice on the dulcimer, so each time is always a new and joyful experience. Because the dulcimer's fretting and modal scales are based on the do-re-mi concept, there are few "wrong" notes, so even people who don't think they have any musical ability can play a simple song beautifully within a short time. Innovative concepts have been added to the modern dulcimer, from chromatic scales to electrification.

However, the basic dulcimer remains a sweet, beautiful, and simple folk instrument.

Once, I was performing and teaching at a four-day dulcimer festival in the Ozarks. There were a few hundred people gathered, and you could hear dulcimer music spilling out from rooms, picnic tables, and campgrounds. Many professional dulcimer builders and players were there, but one player I heard stopped me in my tracks. She was a young girl who was almost hiding in the bushes near the cafeteria. I was passing by and heard the simplest, softest, and most heartfelt sound I had ever heard played. I followed the sound and saw the girl sitting against a wall, playing a new dulcimer she had just bought. The price tag was still hanging from the scroll. I commented on how beautiful her playing was. She blushed and told me she didn't know what she was doing on the instrument because she had never played one before this afternoon. She had just purchased her first dulcimer a few hours before. I was astonished at how sweet her innocence and humbleness sounded. This, to me, is the essence of dulcimer and Dulcimeditation.

Spiritual literature makes a distinction between the higher mind and the ordinary mind and often refers to the ordinary mind as "the monkey mind" or "the baby mind." Our monkey mind often cries like a baby in a crib. How do you quiet a baby in a crib? You wind up a little musical toy hanging over the crib, and soon, the baby stops crying, transfixed by the music. When you sit and play in Dulcimeditation, the music soothes your monkey mind and keeps it occupied, which allows you the space to ask for guidance within. When the monkey mind is transfixed by the music, the usual chatter and inner noise subsides, and the subconscious mind has room to come through.

Playing music, rather than listening to a recording, provides unique effects: you feel the vibration of the dulcimer on your lap and you learn that you can make beautiful music that arises from your very soul…without distress, practice, or reading music. Think of running your fingers gently across wind chimes. It's the same concept. Playing dulcimer is organic, free, and taps into the marvelous muse of creating sweet musical instruments from the wood of trees.

I recorded an album called *Dulcimeditation* with just a dulcimer and the sounds of the Amazon rainforest. It turned out so beautifully that I continue to create new works of Dulcimeditation all the time using various dulcimers in my collection.

I get more clarity throughout the day by simply utilizing Dulcimeditation for five or ten minutes than I ever do sitting with a pen and paper and trying to organize thoughts.

***

"Dulcimeditation"
(Instrumental)
By Kevin Roth

If you would like to hear and experience
Dulcimeditation, go to: KevinRoth.org

Chapter 12
Unconditional Love
—Fur Angels

"Happiness is a warm puppy."
—Charles Schultz

I've learned more about love from my dog Bosco than from any human being I've ever known. I first saw Bosco on Christmas Eve 2013 at a puppy store near my home in Ft. Lauderdale, Florida. There he was, jumping up and down in a baby crib, trying to get my attention while his little brown sister sat beside him, looking tuckered out. Bosco is a small, sweet, dappled miniature dachshund with black, gray, and brown markings over his entire body. His personality melts hearts as his long, wiener body wiggles down the street as he walks me. From the moment I saw him, I knew he was my dog. I had no idea he was my soul mate, too.

A week or so before finding Bosco, I had an OBE experience in which a little dog was running towards me from far away, as if we hadn't seen each other for years. He leapt into my arms, and the lick fest began. I didn't see what type of dog it was, but the feeling of our connection was hard to forget. A few weeks later, when I saw Bosco in the baby crib, I immediately knew he was the dog in my OBE. As big a personality and heart as this eight-week-old love magnet had, he came with an even bigger price tag. As fate would have it, not long before, a little retail store I owned had been broken into and robbed. The only thing they stole was my cash register, which had nothing in it. I had already planned to close the store for good anyway by the end of the following month because I did not enjoy the retail experience, so I took the insurance money I received for the stolen register to pay for Bosco.

On that Christmas Eve, I bought myself the gift of a lifetime. I put his new puppy crate, food, and toys into the back of my jeep, then I put the little guy on my lap and turned on the engine. I'll never forget the look he gave me as he sat on my lap. He stared out the window and then he looked at me as if to say, "Let's get the hell out of here!"

That night he would have nothing to do with sleeping in a crate. It became apparent that the only way I was going to get any sleep was to put him in bed with me. I held him at arm's length, looked into his big brown eyes, and told him, "If you crap in my bed, it'll be the last time we sleep together." He never did, and he's been my bed hog ever since.

Since then, Bosco has been there for me through all my life's ups and downs. In particular, he was there after my nine-year relationship ended, after my father died, and when I closed my store with heavy debt and worry. If I had five dollars for every time someone asked to take a picture of him on their cellphone, I'd have a first-class plane ticket to Paris. The day I was told I had stage 3 melanoma, it was Bosco I held tight as I trembled with fear. He looked at me with those big brown eyes and licked me as if to say, "No matter what happens, we'll get through anything and everything together."

My sister once told me that if I didn't stop posting pictures with "that dog" on Facebook, I would never meet anyone to have a relationship with. I told her I couldn't find anyone as nice as Bosco, so I wasn't concerned. Her comment inspired a song called, "Crazy Love," which I recorded on my album, *The Deviant Dulcimerist*.

Of course, everyone I have spoken to who owns a dog or a cat they love feels the same way about their fur baby. Animals are amazing spiritual souls. They know us better, in a sense, than we know ourselves, and their love is unconditional. All they ask is to be fed and taken care of. That's more than a fair deal, considering what we receive in return. I'll be the first to admit I spoil Bosco. A friend who makes wallets made one for me with Bosco's face on the front, which seemed appropriate since I spend all my spare cash on him, anyway.

Throughout the world dogs are often seen as healing spirits, and their unconditional love can be a source of wisdom and spiritual clarity. Cats, too, have many spiritual connections, but since I'm allergic to them, I can't tell you much from personal experience. My friends seem to love them, and I know cats love sleeping in dulcimer cases. All animals bring balance and hope to the world. Pets are excellent for reducing stress, anxiety, and depression and for easing loneliness. Caring for them teaches children about responsibility and helps them feel more secure and active. They are also wonderful for older adults, as they provide companionship.

A few years ago, I had to take Bosco to the emergency clinic because he had eaten some grapes, which can be lethal for some dogs. They kept him overnight for observation. Those twenty-four hours were difficult for me emotionally. A friend expressed concern that I was too close to Bosco, that if anything happened to him, he worried I'd have a meltdown.

I asked him what he thought I was supposed to do. He suggested I start to distance myself emotionally from Bosco just a little bit, just enough so that I wouldn't be destroyed when the time came that he died. I thought he was nuts. "I'd rather love Bosco every minute of the day and cry my eyes out with sorrow and gratitude when he leaves this planet than be careful emotionally." That incident showed me how some people protect themselves just to avoid being hurt by another human being or the loss of a pet.

For the most part, Bosco and I can look at each other and know what the other is sensing. If I get too heavy in thought, he jumps up and down as if to say, "Get out of your head and lighten up!" Lucky for me, dachshunds can live into their late teens if you keep them healthy. By the time Bosco gets old, I'll be old myself, so who knows? Maybe we could exit the planet together; that would be fine with me. Some people who have had near-death experiences say that they meet loved ones and pets who have passed. I hope that's true. The day I die and reunite with my father and my pets again will be glorious!

I am in large part the man I've become over the years due to Bosco's love and companionship. This book could not have been written without honoring the unique spiritual nature of the animal kingdom, especially my buddy Bosco, who happens to be snoring by my side as I write this chapter.

I share with my students and clients that our pets are part of our healing process. The lessons we learn from them help us to understand the true nature of love. If you don't have a pet, I suggest you consider adopting one if you can. Love is love. It has no gender or identity. It comes in all forms. True love is the essence of who we are and what we long for throughout our entire lives.

***

Crazy Love

Come sweet darling, sit down beside me
I love looking in those eyes
They're big and round and sweet,
colored chocolate brown
Our love was a sweet surprise

Some people say I'm crazy,
maybe, who knows
All I know is I love you, baby,
and I'm glad that it shows
Angels show up in unusual ways
You came along and carried my heart away

When I met you, I was feeling blue
Life was a lonely ride
You know it's darkest before the dawn,
sometimes the light takes so long
But I've got an angel by my side

Some things are meant to be,
like me for you and you for me
Love, it always finds its way
We're a song that must be sung,
our harmonies blend as one
You lighten up my darkest days

Words and Music by Kevin Roth.

Chapter 13
Tuning In to Silence—The Space between the Notes

"One good thing about music, when it
hits you, you feel no pain."
—Bob Marley

W hen I first heard the expression "It's the space between the notes that makes it music," it got me thinking. In musical notation, there are rests which are intervals of silence in pieces of music. Silence allows the rattling of my brain to quiet down long enough that I can listen to what my inner voice is telling me. Like a radio that wasn't quite tuned in to my channel, I lived with more static and fear than clarity, which was exhausting and took its toll. I lived like that for years. Whatever I accomplished in my music career never seemed like enough to me. I never asked myself when enough was enough until I was forced to look at my life after being diagnosed with melanoma. Suddenly the reception came in loud and clear, and the song, "Is That All There Is?" became an anthem. When I changed channels and tuned into silence, my mantra became "Trust Your Gut," which saved my life. If I hadn't taken the time to do deep listening, I would have gone along with some of the bad medical advice I was given from oncologists, and that could have easily ruined my life.

I'm here to tell you that discovering the space between the notes is addicting. It's a high, a freedom that opens stations of the heart and mind you can't even imagine. It's an ongoing experience where you begin to understand what's real in life and what's an illusion. What gave me the impetus to start living this way was when I realized I could be dead within two years and had nothing left to lose.

The choice couldn't have been clearer. I could stay in Kansas waiting to see if the cancer returned while freezing my balls off in the winter, or move to Southern California and play my dulcimer, write, teach, and have fun.

I knew I could become anyone I wanted to be and live anywhere I chose. So, I replaced fear with faith, created a new story for myself, walked right into it, and never looked back.

All my life, music and creativity were my lifeboats. Writing, singing, teaching, and having an outlet to express myself were the oars.

When you hear a song you like, it's the melody and lyrics that grab you, but it's the hook that keeps you coming back for more. In life, the hook is the space. It's who you are on the deepest level. It's reliable, validating, and joyful. It has a good beat, and you can dance to it. William W. Purkey said it best:

*"Dance like nobody's watching, love like you've
never been hurt, sing as though no one can hear
you, live as though heaven is on earth."*

When I wrote the song "Between the Notes" in 2006, I
was living in Fort Lauderdale, Florida, and thinking of
moving to Key West, where many writers who wanted to
be the next Hemingway and vagabond musicians lived.
Although I never moved, I managed to write what a friend
called the ultimate drop-out song. Later, of course, I
realized what I actually needed to do was drop *in*.

***

Between the Notes

*There's a story I once heard of a boy who left home
Before he went he wrote a note by the telephone
It said, I came to this world with nothing,
when I leave I'll take the same
So, I'm off to find the moon and stars
and play celestial games*

*As a man thinketh is he,
it's in the love of what you do
It's the space between the notes,
that makes it music to you*

103

BETWEEN THE NOTES

He said I'm gonna find peace of mind
and a new reality
He shaved his head, lost ten pounds,
ate muffins, and drank green tea
Then he bought a little surf shop
somewhere on the keys
And he lives his days in beautiful ways
down by the turquoise sea

So, here's to all you dreamers
who refuse to stay the same
It's the not the catch it's the chase,
they say, and the loving of the game

Words and music by Kevin Roth.

Section 3

PRACTICAL WAYS TO LIVE IN THE GROOVE

Chapter 14
Integrating Spirituality
—Choices and Balancing Tools

"To know that you are a prisoner of your
mind, that you live in an imaginary world of
your own creation is the dawn of wisdom."
—Nisargadatta Maharaj

The world may be an illusion, and yet we experience it as real; clearly, we experience pain and pleasure. Ramana Maharshi said, "Because we see the world, it is best to accept that one fundamental, which is ourself, is what appears as all this multiplicity."

While I was going through my existential crisis, I had an epiphany: If everything is just a dream or an illusion, then what's the point in getting upset over anything?

To help me maintain balance and happiness while living in the relative world, I developed what I call "choices and balancing tools" for integrating spirituality. When I started to use these consistently, I felt that I had finally laid down my guns and walked away from my own war.

Choices

Every day, in different situations, we choose how to act or react. Here are examples of positive choices I make daily in my own life that you may wish to implement, too:

- Chilling out (Dulcimeditation) instead of feeling stressed

- Contemplation instead of aggravation

- Simplicity instead of complexity

- Fun instead of fear

- Victor instead of victim

These choices may seem obvious and simple, but I discovered that they really worked when I applied them. Life became less dramatic and a lot more fun, and the choices turned into habits. If I catch myself experiencing stress, for example, I can choose to chill out and turn to one of the balancing tools.

Balancing Tools That Work for Me

I use the word *balance* to mean harmony in all the main aspects of the self: emotional, mental, physical, and spiritual. When one part of life is out-of-balance, we are easily thrown off and living is difficult. I use the following tools to keep my life fluid—and happier. I hope that they will inspire you to create your own life-balancing tools.

- When I'm sad or angry (Emotional)— I play music, read something spiritual, hike or exercise to kick in my endorphins, hug my

dog, journal, or talk with someone I know
and trust, someone who will just listen or
offer useful advice. In addition, I have no
hesitation about reaching out for help from
either a life coach or a therapist if I need to.

- When I feel agitated or confused (Mental)—
  I practice gratitude. I find a book or a video
  on the subject in question, which often gives
  me ideas for how to resolve my issues. I do
  Dulcimeditation, which brings me clarity
  and peacefulness. Also, I frequently remind
  myself that *when I change the way I look at
  things, the things I look at change.*

- When I feel blah (Physical)—I make sure I
  get enough sleep, eat well, do intermittent
  fasting, work out, drink enough water, and
  walk in the woods or by the ocean. Being in
  nature always makes me feel grounded and
  healthier, in general. I also know doctors I
  trust and see at least once a year.

- When I need a spiritual perspective
  (Spiritual)—I reconnect with my "source"
  by reading spiritual material that I resonate
  with, meditating (Dulcimeditation),
  reminding myself that life is all an illusion,
  and talking with spiritual friends.

There is a saying I love: Religion is for those who fear hell, and the spiritual is for those who have been there. When people ask me, "What's your religion?" I answer, "The same as God's." I enjoy the teachings of Buddha, Ramana Maharshi, Sufism, Jesus, the Kabbala, and the works of many writers, philosophers, and artists throughout time. There are a lot of paths to the mountain top.

You can find tools that work for you. Look at each aspect of your life—mental, emotional, physical, and spiritual—and think about what you love, what moves you, and what brings you joy. Then, go for it!

A friend recently told me that he envied me. "Why?" I asked.

He said, "You never get upset about things; you never let life beat you down. It's like you're immune to what's going on in the world."

"I choose to be happy every day," I told him, "because I don't like the alternative." Then, I shared a story about my latest dermatology appointment.

The dermatologist said, "Kevin, you have a lot of moles and spots on your body which could very easily turn into melanoma."

I looked at him. "Do I have any signs of cancer, now?"

"No, *not yet.*" I put my shirt back on, looked at him, and said, "So, in other words, I'm cancer-free, keep wearing my sunscreen, you're doing great, Kevin, and see you in a year."

I understood his concerns, but I didn't appreciate his negative projections. So, what did I do? I changed dermatologists and found one who was more optimistic.

Ever since my experience with melanoma, whenever "shit hits the fan," my attitude is, "Well, it ain't cancer." The Serenity Prayer sums up how to maintain a great attitude in life: "God grant me the serenity to accept the things I cannot change, courage to change the things I can, and wisdom to know the difference."

Maintaining Balance

Along with the things I do when I'm feeling out-of-balance, there are certain things I do to *maintain* my balance. I offer them here to you so that you can discover your own.

- Mindful awareness—Being aware of how I'm feeling and what my gut is telling me throughout the day. I check in with myself, adjust my thinking when needed, and then I go with the flow.

- Simply being—I sit down with a cup of coffee or tea in a quiet place, and just be. No cellphones, emails, messages, work, or planning. I quiet my mind and relax. The world will be there when I get back to it.

- Spending time with my dog, Bosco—The joy and the unconditional love of playing with Bosco is the best therapy I know. If you don't have a pet, consider getting one or spending time with a friend who does!

- Enjoying the mystery—Thinking about the connection between spirituality and science keeps me in awe. It reminds me that everything is simply a dream at play.

- Being grateful—I practice gratitude every day. I'm grateful I'm healthy, I'm grateful people enjoy my music, I adore my dog, I'm able to do what I love, and I love what I do.

Every so often, I drive to a place called Idyllwild for a change of scenery. It's a beautiful mountain town about two hours from San Diego that has amazing hiking and views. The "outer view" of being in nature changes my "inner view" every time. I rented a tiny cabin in the woods there once, and while sitting on the small porch with Bosco curled up beside me, I wrote an instrumental piece that I recorded and named "Idyllwild." Tapping into the musical muse is one of my favorite ways to stay grounded and happy, especially when instrumentals come to me in beautiful places with the scent of pine trees in the air.

***

"Idyllwild"
(Dulcimer instrumental)
Music by Kevin Roth.

This instrumental, along with all the other songs in this book, can be found on the album *Songs from the Book Between the Notes,* which is available at:
KevinRothMusic.com

Chapter 15
Kevin's Creative Life Design
—Creating Your Story

"Keep it simple, keep it honest, keep it real."
—Anonymous

I knew a musician who came home from an out-of-town gig a day early and found his wife in bed with another man. He told me he was not only hurt, but he felt like a loser. He had gotten into arguments with his wife over the years about his not having a "real job," about him getting fat, and about their constant struggle to make ends meet even with two jobs.

A few years later, I hired him to play on a new album, and when he walked into the recording studio, I hardly recognized him. He had lost at least fifty pounds, his scruffy look had been replaced by a short haircut, and he walked with an air of confidence about him. I asked him how he had lost weight and about his new dapper look. He told the story about finding his wife in bed with another man and the transformation he underwent.

He said, "Finding my wife with that guy and her telling me later, 'You got what you deserved, asshole,' was the greatest thing she ever did for me. I left her, enrolled in college to become a mechanical engineer, and I'm now earning six figures. I have a new wife and a baby."

I was amazed. Talk about changing your story!

The most important step in creating a new story for yourself is developing the ability to love and respect yourself. If you don't know you deserve to be happy, you will never truly be able to change.

All of us can change our story at any time. I experienced changing my own story when I moved from Kansas to California, which I've written about throughout this book. I also know people who finally *decided it was time* to change their lives because "enough was enough." They walked out of abusive relationships or changed jobs or lost weight or changed environments. They began new lives by being clear about what they wanted and didn't want and by understanding that life is not a dress rehearsal. It's your God-given right to be happy. I have found that certain questions are helpful as you create your new story, and I cover these in the next chapter.

Creating your new story includes those with whom you associate. This is especially true for your intimate relationship. Does your partner support you? If you're single, do you "need" someone to make you feel loved, or can you love yourself? Of course, if you happen to meet the right person, that's icing on the cake.

Beware. Cupid throws us curve balls every once in a while.

Love

The story about love is always an interesting one, isn't it? It's a rare occasion when I meet someone I think I could fall in love with. So, when I met Pat, who turned my world upside-down, I was dizzy and thrilled. After a few days and many hours spent talking while gazing into each other's eyes, Pat said, "Umm, I have a few pets." I was thinking something like two dogs and a cat, and I also wondered why this topic hadn't come up earlier. Pat certainly knew about Bosco.

There was a long pause, and a cautious look on Pat's face. Then, I was shown a plethora of photographs of the "pets." They included roly-poly bugs, lizards, snakes, turtles, a tortoise, frogs, toads, fishes, crawfish, dubia roaches, a tarantula, cockroaches, ferrets, and a hamster. I kid you not!

My first reaction was a kind of daze; I had no idea that I had begun to fall in love with Dr. Doolittle. My second thought? Well, there was no way in hell I was going to live with a ferret named "Stanley" sitting next to me while watching Netflix, no matter how "cute" and "friendly" it was. Okay, maybe the frog, the turtle, and some fish.

When I said I didn't want to get involved with "Noah's Ark," I was given that old line about compromise being part of a healthy relationship. I was reminded that, like Bosco, these pets were family.

In the past, I would have "managed" to compromise and live with part of the animal kingdom in my living room. But now I know where my boundaries are and what makes me happy. Noah's Ark is outside the boundary line. So, I told "Dr. Doolittle" that I understood and respected that this "animal kingdom" was important, and then I suggested that we just be friends.

I always tell my clients that for a relationship to work for both people, it first must work for each individually. Your new story begins with loving and respecting yourself, knowing your boundaries and never depending on anyone else to make you happy. Happiness is a choice. Unless there is a circumstance that's out of your control, you can always change your story.

When I changed my story and learned to make myself happy, I was happier around other people. When I learned to love myself first, I was able to give love to others. This is not a selfish act; it's about self-respect and wanting the best for you and for those around you. I didn't hesitate over that decision. It felt good to know that I was perfectly content on my own. I didn't need to compromise. Of course, I do think compromise is valid and important once you're already *in a relationship*.

Before I changed my story, I gave my joy and sanity away to other people, victimhood, depression, feeling stuck, and always seeking validation for what I felt and thought. My old story ended with my death sentence. In a strange way, part of me died in Kansas, and I was happy to see it go. My new story started the day I walked into my apartment after being told I had cancer and said to myself out loud, "Don't worry, buddy, we'll get through this." And "we" did. I like being my own bestie. I'm not suggesting being self-centered, but rather soul- and heart-centered. Authentic.

In terms of falling in love, there's a lid for every pot. In addition to menageries, I also don't care for cigarettes or drama, and of course, if ya don't like Bosco, well, pack your bags!

The Day Kevin Died

We never know how much our lives affect other people. Of all the strange experiences I've had in my life, nothing beats the time in my mid-twenties when I got to witness others' reactions to my own assumed death.

I was giving a concert in Philadelphia at The Painted Bride Arts Center. I had a terrible stiff neck that week, and, for some reason, a weird sense that I was going to die. I had asked my friend Roy to come with me to the show and told him about my concern. Roy knew that I'd had precognitive experiences before, so he wasn't too surprised. My stiff neck was so bad that I had to angle the piano differently on stage so I could turn my neck to see the audience.

After the show, we drove home, and on the way, we ran into a sleet storm that made driving hazardous. We drove thirty miles an hour so as not to slide off the road, and finally arrived at my place around one thirty in the morning. When we got in, the phone rang. "Who the hell would call me at one thirty in the morning?" I thought to myself. It was a woman from a local hospital looking for Kevin Roth's parents. I told her I was Kevin Roth, and there was a long silence. Then, she told me she was calling to inform his family that there had been a car accident, and Kevin had been killed along with his friend that evening. When I told Roy about the call, he said, "Oh man!" We both just stood there in shock.

I had been living next door to my father at the time. The next morning, my father woke me up. He said, "I wanted to be sure you were alive. Neighbors are coming over to pay their condolences because it's on the news that you were killed." I discovered that WXPN radio in Philadelphia had started playing my music in memoriam. My friends were calling each other and crying. The whole thing was so bizarre that neither Roy nor I knew what to make of it all.

Someone had picked up my business card and given it to another Kevin Roth, who lived in the same area. He had put my card inside his wallet, which is how the hospital contacted me after matching the name with his driver's license. I heard his neck was broken in the accident, which explained my stiff neck on the day of my gig at The Painted Bride, just before the accident. I was so freaked out by the whole thing that I pushed away all precognitive experiences for about a year. I refused to pay attention.

Within the next week or so, I witnessed how much my music meant to people. I had no idea. I never even thought my friends cared about me so much. It was an eye-opener.

The reason I'm sharing this experience is to tell you what I learned firsthand:

The story you create for your life affects not only you but those around you in ways you can't even imagine.

People may not remember the things you said, but they usually remember how you made them feel.

Steps for Creating Your New Story (Kevin's Creative Life Design)

These are the steps I took to let go of my past and design a life I loved. As I did so, I created a new vision that became my "story" moving forward. I invite you to make use of them to create your own new story.

- **Focus on what matters**. Become absolutely clear about what matters to you and why.

- **Create a game plan**. With that clarity, set a plan for the steps you need to take to make your dream a reality. I did this by researching what had worked for other people who had changed their lives.

- **Research**. Google anything and everything related to your mission. Read what other people have done to accomplish their mission; it will encourage you and give you more ideas. Feel excited about your vision, and remember, activity breeds activity.

- **Never, ever give up**. If you want to make a change badly enough, you'll figure out a way. Where there's a will, there's a way. I'm living proof!

- **Act "as if."** Act as if your dream is already happening. For example, when I decided to move to California, I began throwing away things I didn't need or want to take with me. I got boxes and began to pack. Although I had no idea where I would move, I put the *action of moving* into motion. Seeing it and believing it made it real.

- **Plan your new story**. Plan your new story as if you are planning a vacation. Ask yourself where you want to go, when, how much it cost, what you will do, and so on. If you do this thoroughly, you'll never work another day in your life. Why? Because when you love what you do, it doesn't feel like work.

- **Take responsibility**. Ask for help when you need it, but never rely on other people to make it happen. I took 100 percent control. I was the undisputed author of my story.

- **Adjust**. When something doesn't feel right along the way, use your mindful awareness for clarity, and be willing to adjust your plans and figure out a way to make your new life story work for you. Nothing in life is permanent. Be willing to go with the flow if it feels right.

- **Trust your gut**. This is imperative, especially with doctors, "experts," and—in my case—music industry people. I'm referring to anyone who tells you such and such is the way it is and if you don't believe them, you'll regret not heeding their advice. Listen, do your research, come to your own conclusions, and never let the opinions of others stop you.

- **Have faith**. Even if you are not religious, trust what you do believe and surrender to your inner voice/guidance. I am not religious, but I believe in God/Consciousness within the dream world, so I always trust it and surrender, allowing myself to be guided towards the right decisions.

And here is the most important piece of all, the major factor in making your new life story real:

- **Believe and KNOW**, allowing no doubt, that this dream is yours. And if it doesn't work out, at least you will die trying.

If you take only one thing away from this book, take this, because it is worth a fortune:

YOUR THOUGHTS ARE POWERFUL!

Chapter 16

11 Powerful Life Questions for Your Creative Life Design

"Ask the right questions if you're to find the right answers."
—Vanessa Redgrave

B ack in Kansas, when I was trying to figure out how to reinvent my life, I asked myself some basic questions. I gathered a long list of answers which, in turn, produced further questions. I sifted through all of them until I narrowed them down to the most important ones.

I tossed these questions around in my head for weeks, taking into consideration how they made me feel emotionally, mentally, spiritually, and physically. The word *feel* is huge; if you don't *feel* good about your decisions, you're not going to be "all in," and then you end up living a half-hearted life. After about a month of thinking things through, digging into my feelings, and writing down my answers, I became crystal-clear about how I wanted my future to look.

Kevin's Creative Life Design

As my new life unfolded, I found that the process was a lot like building a house. You first must establish the foundation, and then you build the frame and interior sections. The questions I was pondering correlated with key elements of building a house. There are four key areas:

- **Foundation:** Knowing what matters represents the foundation.

- **Framework:** Knowing why it matters is the framework.

- **Interior:** What to do about the things that matter is the process of building the interior.

- **Decoration:** You create a life you love by decorating your "inner rooms" with fun and authentic ideas that resonate with your being. I call it creative life design.

Don't put off your dreams until some later date. Life is not a dress rehearsal. Believe me when I tell you: *life can change on a dime.* If you can't make changes right now, at least get your dreams cooking! I tell my students and clients: "Remember, activity breeds activity." Set your dreams in motion by acting on them. Even if you take only one or two small steps, everything you manage to do adds up.

For this process, I suggest you get a notebook and write down each question and then your answer, making sure that fear and negativity do not enter the equation. For example, one of my questions was, "Where do you want to live?" I wrote: "I want to move to California and live there." Immediately, thoughts popped up, like, "Oh, you can't afford to live in California!" I noticed this and replaced "I want to live there" with "I'm *going* to live there!" and so I found a way! There is power in making decisions, committing to them, and not letting anything stand in your way.

This may sound odd, but don't give in to logic. Just because something doesn't make sense or seems extraordinary, if you really want it, go for it! At the beginning of my dulcimer career, I was told to learn the guitar instead, because nobody knew what a dulcimer was. I didn't listen. Instead, I followed my heart, and it worked to my advantage.

Also, don't give in to the fear of what others may say. Be original. Everybody has a unique talent inside, whether it's in business or the arts. Here is one of my favorite sayings:

> **"Blessed are the weird people: poets, misfits, writers, mystics, painters, troubadours for they teach us to see the world through different eyes."**
> —Jacob Nordby

Sometimes being too concerned about what other people may think if you step "out of the box" and be original can inhibit your creativity. When I began to play the dulcimer, I did very unconventional things with it. I saw the dulcimer as a canvas to paint on. The traditional folkies didn't care for my style, but in the end, I became renowned for being an "innovative dulcimer player."

Whenever I have doubts about moving in a new direction, I am reminded of an inspirational video of a guy in San Diego who wanted to play the guitar. He had no arms, so he learned to play with his feet. His video is on YouTube: "Amazing guitarist playing only with his feet in Balboa Park, San Diego." It is a wonderful reminder that people are turning "impossible" into "I'm possible" every day, and you can, too.

You are the author of your own life. If you want to be happy and successful, you need to be clear about these two things:

- **What you *don't* want in your life.**

- **What you *do* want in your life.**

Top 11 Powerful Life Questions

Here are the questions from which I gained insight. Answering them helped my life, and I hope they may help you, as well. Be honest with your thoughts and feelings as you answer these questions. No one is judging you except you. Take the time you need to define and get clear on what your dream life looks and feels like. If you take time for some introspective work as you answer these questions, you will be amazed at the outcome.

1. What really matters to you?

2. Why does it matter?

3. How will you feel when you obtain your dream?

4. What will your life feel and look like when this happens?

5. How will you feel if you don't try to make your dream happen?

6. What are the things you think are holding you back, and what can you do about them?

7. Are you happy in your environment, and if not, where would you prefer to live?

8. How is your health, and what needs to improve?

9. What's your game plan to make these changes in your life?

10. Where can you find supportive, inspiring people (mentors) you can talk to or read about?

11. Imagine you're on your death bed, looking back over your life: what do you wish you had done differently or changed?

These questions may seem simple but keep inquiring into them and journaling about what you find and you will gain profound insights.

What to Do When You Hit a Wall
(Handling the Monkey Mind)

We all experience emotional ups and downs and situations when we need to step back, take a breath, and try to find clarity. Truth to tell, this is all about the monkey mind playing with ya! "Monkey mind" is a Buddhist term. It refers to being unsettled, restless, confused, and the like. To help you manage the shenanigans of the monkey mind, let's look at four specific areas: procrastination, ambivalence, fear, and feeling stuck, all of which can combine in troublesome ways.

Procrastination

We procrastinate in making decisions and changes because we're either ambivalent, fearful, or feeling stuck in our journey. One day, I realized I was procrastinating over a major life decision I was trying to make. I went hiking. I thought to myself, "You teach this stuff; for God's sake, Kevin, how can you possibly be feeling like this? And also, why can't you allow yourself to feel stuck occasionally?"

I did a small coaching session on myself and concluded that I'm human, too! That made me dig deeper into understanding myself. I discovered I was being hard on myself because I wanted to know the answer—*now!* I wanted to feel in control *immediately!* The truth is, everything constantly evolves, and in a way, the greatest control in life is the lack of it. I needed to let go of control, to let go of this desire to find immediate gratification. Seeing this, I gave up the struggle. I realized that the answer would come naturally and at the appropriate time. Don't force anything. When you swim against the current, it's always difficult. When you go with the flow, you find your way naturally.

Ambivalence

Ambivalence is a state of having mixed feelings about something or someone. I had a friend who used the expression, "I do, but I don't," when asked if he wanted to do things like, for instance, go to dinner. It drove me crazy. He lived in a world of constant ambivalence. Committing to do anything was a process for him, except when it came to his job. Eventually, I stopped asking him to do anything with me.

A student recently told me that she "kind of, sort of" wanted to change her living situation, something she had been thinking about for over a year. "What will it take for you to decide? Maybe you're simply not in enough pain or discomfort to make changes in your life right now."

Her roommate finally moved out, which solved that particular problem for her.

Sigmund Freud suggested that people make life choices based on either pain or pleasure. Think about it. Why be in pain if you can work through your feelings and feel more pleasure? What helps if you're feeling ambivalent? Find answers, stop judging yourself, make decisions, and act.

Fear

Fear can freeze people in their tracks. Next time this happens to you, explore what is happening. Ask yourself, "What am I afraid *of?*" Most of the time, you may find that you are simply making a fearful projection about the future. Remember, FEAR stands for False Evidence Appearing Real. Fear can easily lead to ambivalence. I often must remind myself: *The past is gone and the future isn't here, so stay in the present moment.* This is where mindful awareness really comes into play. As you work through fear, you create more space in your head and find more energy to do things you love. Opposites of fear are curiosity, trust, courage, and acceptance.

Fear can present an incredible opportunity for turning your life completely around in a positive way. One night, I went to see my favorite musical group and friends Peter, Paul & Mary perform at the Valley Forge Music Fair. At the time, they were the most popular folk group in the world. I had just come from giving my own concert earlier that afternoon, so I had my dulcimer with me. While sitting in Mary's dressing room, she invited me to perform a song during her solo part of the show. Her friend Mike Renshaw and I had written it together. It was about the homeless and was called "No Forwarding Address." I adored Mary. I couldn't believe she was asking me to solo during a Peter, Paul and Mary show! I think I was one of only two people who ever did a solo guest appearance during one of their concerts.

When Mary introduced me, I thought I would pass out—literally. I was scared to death and excited all at the same time. I went on stage, sat down, and began to sing while Mary sat at my feet on stage. I was in heaven. A friend at the show photographed Mary and me on stage together. I have a cassette of the performance. At the end, Mary said, "You did good!" What a blast! I put that photo on a coffee mug and looked at it for years, always thinking, "Man, if *that could happen, anything can happen*! So, let go of fear and go for it! You, too, may gain a memory that you treasure every single day.

Feeling Stuck

In my experience, feeling stuck is due to a lack of clarity. When you feel in a rut and unclear about what to do, the first step is to identify what needs to change. What really matters? Why does it matter? Go back to the 11 Questions. If I have gone through this process and still feel stuck, I ask myself: What do I no longer want in my life?

When I first moved back to California, I wanted to make new friends. I sat on this idea for quite a while, doing nothing, until I realized I felt stuck when I tried to figure out how to go about it. When I analyzed why, suddenly, making new friends was a problem, I discovered I was projecting a negative outcome: I might not find the right fit. In a sense, fear had led me to feel ambivalent. What did I really want? I identified that I really wanted to meet *artistic people*. That was true clarity. Soon, I found a meet-up group for artists and film buffs and met several new friends.

Creating a life you love comes down to this: What do you want? what don't you want? and what are you going to do about it? The 11 Questions will guide you to getting unstuck, dropping fear, and putting a stop to procrastination. You may discover that the real reason you are procrastinating is that you really don't want to do "X" at all!

Remember:

- *"When you change the way that you look at things, the things you look at change."*
—Wayne Dyer

- *"When you replace what doesn't work with what does, you never go back."*
—Kevin Roth

Chapter 17
The Art of Love and Happiness

"Happiness is a choice, not a result.
Nothing will make you happy until you
<u>choose to be happy</u>.
No person will make you happy unless you
<u>decide to be happy</u>.
Your happiness will not come to you.
<u>It can only come from you</u>."
—Ralph Marston

By 2016, I knew that it was imperative to me to create a life I loved, a life that was authentic and meaningful. I figured out the practical things that worked, which I've shared within this book, including:

- What truly mattered to me
- Why it mattered on a deep soul level
- What I was going to do about it
- Learning to love myself
- Rewriting my new playbook and walking right into it

As the saying goes, "It works if you work it." With exuberance, I worked it and landed on my feet, dancing to the beat of my own muse-ical song in life. But when it came to fully integrating my spiritual knowledge into my life, there still seemed to be a missing piece.

> *"Love isn't an emotion or an instinct—it's an art."*
> —Mae West

Practical Spirituality

Within the first week or two of moving to San Diego, I drove four hours up to Ojai to get some answers from my teacher and friend, author Robert Wolfe, about practical spirituality. I said, "Self-realization and *Ajata* are wonderful and fascinating, but so what?"

I had three questions about self-realization:

- What do you do with it?

- How will it make a real difference in my life on a day-to-day level?

- How is it integrated into the dream experience?

Following is what he told me in a nutshell, and I have experienced it to be true over time. These discoveries fundamentally changed my life for the better. I'm sharing them with you because, eventually, you will discover that this is where the rubber meets the road. I found that when I incorporated these ideas, which I call my spiritual soup for the soul, I reframed my life in a way that was freeing.

- **Integrate your self-realization**: By following the concepts and understandings that I have realized and integrating them into my daily life, I've experienced a shift in my awareness and how I live my daily life. Gradually, this resulted in a change of values for me spiritually, as well as in my business and personal life. These days, my "role" matches my "soul."

- **Let go of drama**: I no longer engage in the endless speculations and conflicts that interested me before. For example, I don't get into lengthy political, religious, or economic discussions about things like whether my Social Security benefits will be there for me when I need them or whether the world is coming to an end soon. I save the drama for plays. I take it one day at a time. My life is far more peaceful as a result.

- **Recognize that life is impermanent**: Now that I realize how impermanent everything is, my thoughts are no longer a huge problem. Everything changes. Nothing stays the same. This has helped me learn how to control my monkey mind instead of letting it control me.

- **Know that we are all actors in the movie of life**: This "dream life" continues to be my experience within the "dream world," but how I relate to it has changed. I live my life as if I'm an actor in a movie. I look at whatever

comes and goes as just scenes within the
movie. This keeps things light, fun, and
incredibly interesting.

We all desire love and happiness. You could say that finding and keeping is a subtle art form. "Like fractals expanding in an infinite dance, it's all an inside job." We're like musical instruments that need to be slightly retuned each time they're played. We need constant retuning because love and happiness certainly have ups and downs. The trick is not getting so badly out of tune that we feel like we have to start from square one. Keep mindful awareness humming along, and you will need only a few adjustments to be in harmony. I think about this often when I sit down with my dulcimer and do Dulcimeditation.

I recently remarked to a friend, "The way I live now, who needs psychedelics? If you were to crawl inside my head, you'd wonder what I was taking." The life I'm living didn't happen overnight. As I've said before, meaningful change is a slow-drip process, but it yields rich results. So, be gentle with yourself. Use the tools and ideas I've shared and see how they work for you. My students and clients who have used them report that they handle stress better, they have more energy, they have way more fun, and life in general has taken on a childlike wonder.
Most important, we are often too hard on ourselves. Therefore, it is crucial to learn to love yourself.

"You yourself, as much as anybody in the entire universe, deserve your love and affection."
—Buddha

Conclusion
Reflecting, Resonating, and Remembering

"A day will dawn when you will laugh at your past efforts. What you realize on the day you laugh is also here and now."
—Ramana Maharshi

Taking positive action on the information I've provided in this book is the most rewarding work you'll ever do. You will scratch your head and wonder why you ever acted the way you did in the past. When you feel your life change for the better, you'll discover it's the only game in town. Automatically, certain actions will become wonderful new habits because they keep your life simple, easy, and humming along. As I've said before, when you replace *what doesn't work* in your life with *what does work*, you never go back!

The following five habits are the *crème de la crème* of how I keep my life in harmony and humming along:

- **Trust your gut.** Learn to tune in to what your inner voice is saying, and always trust your gut.

141

- **Release stress.** Remember that stress and inflammation help suppress your immune system, allowing the possibility of cancer and other diseases to emerge.

- **Follow your bliss.** Find out where your song lives and crawl into it.

- **Don't step in it.** Yes, that's exactly what I mean. When you start to get into drama or see a situation that smells like trouble, avoid it.

- **Use your balancing tools.** There's always something you can do to calm the monkey mind. Once you get familiar with what works for you, use it, and remember that you're the one holding the banana!

I teach from my experience; only that. I may read or hear something that seems great, but until I experience it myself, I don't feel I can effectively teach it to anyone else. Why? Because there's "book learning" and "street learning." Book learning is abstract, while street learning is up close and personal. As far as I'm concerned, the best mentors in life are those who have figured out what's what and walk the talk. Of course, we never figure everything out within this dream experience, but nuggets of real gold are better than fake gems.

The most rewarding part of doing workshops, retreats, and personal sessions is watching others discover their own Aha! moments. New possibilities unfold right before their eyes. And our discussions about spirituality, balance, choices, dreams, and so on, are always fascinating. I love to see someone's face change as they move from feeling stressed, stuck, and confused at the beginning of a session to relieved, joyful, and clear by the end.

I believe everything happens for a reason. I often hear from people who have seen or heard me somewhere. They tell me how happy they were to "find me," that they resonated with something I had said. I'm not surprised. I give people permission to be themselves without judgment or criticism. Many people say they were looking for spiritual solutions to their lives and were grateful to hear about my journey. Of course, I've heard from many folks who battle cancer or who wanted to rewrite their stories but didn't know how. We're all on a journey together. Your journey is not all that different from mine.

We all wonder why we came into this world, what our life purpose is, and what will happen when we die.

Recently, someone asked me what had prompted me to write this book. In a way, I wanted closure on a long chapter in my life because I felt that a wonderful, brand-new chapter was beginning. I also thought back to when my friend told me I should be a life coach, and what he said when I asked him why. When he told me that the experiences I went through could really help others, my first reaction was to dismiss him. I was a songwriter, not a teacher. Then, the muse got ahold of me, and I followed it. What else could I do? It's my nature.

> *"Tomorrow is a mystery. Today is a gift.*
> *That's why we call it The Present."*
> —Eleanor Roosevelt

I hope my journey and the insights I have shared help you discover your own inner groove and dance to a beat that makes your heart sing.

Build your own *creative life design* as if your life depends on it—because it does!

About the Author

Kevin Roth is an internationally known dulcimer player, singer, songwriter, and recording artist. His recording career began in 1974 with the prestigious folk music label Folkways Records/Smithsonian, where he recorded fourteen albums. In 1984, Kevin started  recording award-winning children's music on his own label. He sang the theme song for the hit PBS television show, *Shining Time Station,* and composed and performed several music videos, gaining millions of fans worldwide. Kevin has recorded fifty-one albums of dulcimer music, including *Dulcimeditation.* He has performed around the world and has won numerous awards.

In 2014, Kevin was diagnosed with stage 3 melanoma and was told that although the melanoma had been removed, there was a 70 percent chance it would return within a year and that he would be dead within three years. Hearing these words prompted Kevin to begin an earnest spiritual search for the true meaning in his life. He changed his diet and his attitude and created a new story for a happy and cancer-free life.

In 2020, Kevin created "Dulcimeditation" and began coaching individuals on how they, too, could reduce stress, stop feeling stuck, and learn how to create a life they loved using the techniques he developed.

Kevin now combines his music and his incredible story of resilience in an entertaining presentation that he delivers as a keynote speaker, in workshops, and as a retreat leader. He guides people from all walks of life in how to create a life of fun, health, happiness, and lasting meaning.

Kevin lives in San Diego, California, with his dog Bosco, his collection of dulcimers, and his own original artwork.

To book Kevin for speaking to your group, for workshops, or for consulting, please visit his website where you will learn more about him, dulcimers, and courses.

KevinRoth.org

All the songs in this book, can be found on the album
SONGS FROM THE BOOK BETWEEN THE NOTES.

For information on Kevin's music, visit:
KevinRothMusic.com

Made in USA - Crawfordsville, IN
35965_9781957343082
01.27.2023 1043